CAMPAIGN 347

CONSTANTINOPLE AD 717–18

The Crucible of History

SI SHEPPARD ILLUSTRATED BY GRAHAM TURNER

Series editor Marcus Cowper

OSPREY PUBLISHING
Bloomsbury Publishing Plc
PO Box 883, Oxford, OX1 9PL, UK
1385 Broadway, 5th Floor, New York, NY 10018, USA
E-mail: info@ospreypublishing.com
www.ospreypublishing.com

OSPREY is a trademark of Osprey Publishing Ltd

First published in Great Britain in 2020

A catalogue record for this book is available from the British Library.

ISBN: PB 9781472836922; eBook 9781472836939; ePDF 9781472836908; XML 9781472836915

20 21 22 23 24   10 9 8 7 6 5 4 3 2 1

Maps by Bounford.com
3D BEVs by the Black Spot
Index by Nick Hayhurst
Typeset by PDQ Digital Media Solutions, Bungay, UK
Printed and bound in India by Replika Press Private Ltd.

Artist's note

Readers may care to note that the original paintings from which the colour plates in this book were prepared are available for private sale. All reproduction copyright whatsoever is retained by the publishers. All enquiries should be addressed to:

Graham Turner, PO Box 568, Aylesbury, Bucks. HP17 8ZX UK
www.studio88.co.uk

The publishers regret that they can enter into no correspondence upon this matter.

Osprey Publishing supports the Woodland Trust, the UK's leading woodland conservation charity.

To find out more about our authors and books visit **www.ospreypublishing.com**. Here you will find extracts, author interviews, details of forthcoming events and the option to sign up for our newsletter.

Dedication

To James Sheppard – my taller, better-looking, and much wiser younger brother.

Key to military symbols

xxxxx	xxxx	xxx	xx	x	III	II
Army Group	Army	Corps	Division	Brigade	Regiment	Battalion

				Key to unit identification
I				
Company/Battery	Infantry	Artillery	Cavalry	Unit identifier / Parent unit / Commander / (+) with added elements / (–) less elements

PREVIOUS PAGE
The walls of Constantinople.

CONTENTS

The ascent of Islam, 622–750/51

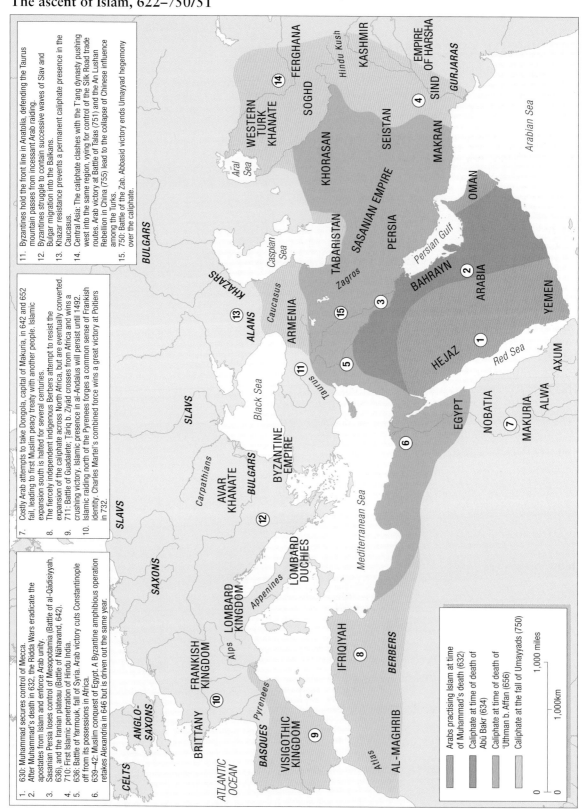

1. 630: Muhammad secures control of Mecca.
2. After Muhammad's death in 632, the Ridda Wars eradicate the apostates from Islam and enforce Arab unity.
3. Sasanian Persia loses control of Mesopotamia (Battle of al-Qādisiyyah, 636), and the Iranian plateau (Battle of Nāhavand, 642).
4. 710: First Islamic penetration of Hindu India.
5. 636: Battle of Yarmouk. Arab victory cuts Constantinople off from its possessions in Syria.
6. 639–42: Muslim conquest of Egypt. A Byzantine amphibious operation retakes Alexandria in 646 but is driven out the same year.
7. Costly Arab attempts to take Dongola, capital of Makuria, in 642 and 652 fail, leading to first Muslim peacy treaty with another people. Islamic expansion south is halted for several centuries.
8. The fiercely independent indigenous Berbers attempt to resist the expansion of the caliphate across North Africa, but are eventually converted.
9. 711: Battle of Guadalete: Tāriq b. Ziyād crosses from Africa and wins a crushing victory. Islamic victory, fall of al-Andalus will persist until 1492.
10. Islamic raiding north of the Pyrenees forges a common sense of Frankish identity. Charles Martel's combined force wins a great victory at Poitiers in 732.
11. Byzantines hold the front line in Anatolia, defending the Taurus mountain passes from incessant Arab raiding.
12. Byzantines struggle to contain successive waves of Slav and Bulgar migration into the Balkans.
13. Khazar resistance prevents a permanent caliphate presence in the Caucasus.
14. Central Asia: The caliphate clashes with the T'ang dynasty pushing west into the same region, vying for control of the Silk Road trade routes. Arab victory at Battle of Talas (751) and the An Lushan Rebellion in China (755) lead to the collapse of Chinese influence among the Turks.
15. 750: Battle of the Zab. Abbasid victory ends Umayyad hegemony over the caliphate.

Arabs practising Islam at time of Muhammad's death (632)

Caliphate at time of death of Abū Bakr (634)

Caliphate at time of death of 'Uthmān b. Affan (656)

Caliphate at the fall of Umayyads (750)

0   1,000 miles

0   1,000km

ORIGINS OF THE CAMPAIGN

In the year 626, Constantinople, the capital city of what history has dubbed the Byzantine Empire, was brought under siege for the first time.

Over the seven decades since the Nika insurrection of 532 the inhabitants of the great metropolis had enjoyed peace. But in 602, the imperial armies on the Danube frontier had rebelled, marched on Constantinople, murdered the emperor, Maurice, and installed one of their own, Phocas, in his stead. What ensued was catastrophic. In the west, the Avars and Slavs rumbled across the exposed border and overran the Balkans. In the east, Khosrow II, shah of the Sasanian dynasty of Persia, declared war. A new emperor, Heraclius, had seized the throne in 610, but the tide was running against him. Jerusalem had fallen in 614, the Sasanians bearing the True Cross in triumph back to their capital, Ctesiphon. In 619, the last functioning imperial mint, at Nicomedia, was forced to abandon coin production, and Alexandria, the last imperial stronghold in Egypt, fell, cutting Constantinople off from its source of grain; the bread ration (*annona*) for the population of the city was cancelled.

Heraclius had written to Khosrow, urging him to choose peace: 'Let us quench this fire before it consumes everything.' But the war approached its climax in 626. At the start of the summer campaign season, a Sasanian army crossed the Taurus Mountains and marched unimpeded through Asia Minor to Chalcedon, across the Bosporus from Constantinople. Their intent was to serve as the anvil in support of their Avar allies as they delivered the hammer blow against the city.

The Avars had mobilized a huge army, which included their Slav clients; the total of 80,000 men given by George of Pisidia can be corroborated by the figure of 30,000 given in the *Chronicon Paschale* for the vanguard which approached Constantinople on 29 June. The Bosporus was illuminated on both shores by the flames of burning suburbs that day as the Avars commenced the blockade of Constantinople on its landward side. The sunlight 'reflected its rays on their steel,' Theodore Syncellus wrote, 'and showed them still more terrible, making those who looked at them shiver with fear.' Morale was already shaky, for the emperor was not in his city; still on campaign deep in Sasanian territory, Heraclius had deputed the defence to the Patriarch, Sergius, and the patrician, Bonus.

The empire had been reduced to its core, but it still had one trump card: the capital itself. Geography had blessed the site with natural advantages that made it the most secure in the world.

During the long reign of Khosrow II (r. 590, 591–628), depicted on this silver drachma, Sasanian Persia both reached its greatest territorial extent and suffered its most crushing defeat. His armies overran Syria and Egypt, but when Heraclius broke into the Sasanian heartland after a quarter of a century of war, it broke the Sasanian will to keep up the fight. Khosrow was overthrown by his own son, Kavad II, who murdered him in February 628. The period of chaotic political disequilibrium following his death led to the complete collapse of the Sasanian state to the Arab jihad. (Noble Numismatics, https://www.noble.com.au/)

Constantinople occupied a peninsula that was bordered on two sides by open water. To the south lay the Sea of Marmara. To the north was the inlet of the Golden Horn. The approach by land from the west was closed off by the triple line of the Theodosian walls. These state-of-the-art fortifications had never been challenged, let alone breached; even Attila the Hun had turned back when he laid eyes on them. Now they would be put to the test.

The Avar khagan arrived with the main army on 29 July. The Avars swiftly set to assembling siege machines, using their own wagons and timber stripped from buildings in the suburbs as construction material. On 31 July, a total of 12 siege towers, matching the height of the ramparts, were deployed and the attack opened along the whole length of the Theodosian walls. The fighting would continue every day until the end of the siege, the main effort being concentrated against the central section in the low ground of the Lycus Valley.

The noose tightened. A fleet of Slav boats (which had been transported overland) was launched, on the fourth day of the siege, at the head of the Golden Horn, compelling the defenders to deploy a cordon of warships to prevent them from reaching the sea walls. Three envoys from the Persians also succeeded in slipping across the Bosporus, but the following day they were intercepted making their way back to Chalcedon. On Sunday 3 August, the Byzantines sent the enemy a message of their own. One of the envoys, minus his hands, but with the head of a second envoy suspended from his neck, was presented to the khagan. The third envoy was taken by boat and beheaded in full view of the Persian army.

That evening, the transport vessels which the khagan had launched on the Bosporus north of the city earlier in the day succeeded in evading the 70 Roman warships sent to blockade them, and crossed over to the Persians. It was now feasible for the Persians to send troops across, and even a token detachment would be of great symbolic value. Sebeos reports that a large Persian force was dispatched, only to be intercepted and defeated by a Roman fleet.

Events were now approaching a climax. There was no let-up in the pressure during the sixth, seventh and eighth days of the siege (Sunday 3 August to Tuesday 5 August) while preparations were made for a general assault.

Skirmishing and local attacks kept the defenders under pressure and the number of siege engines continued to grow. On Wednesday 6 August (the ninth day of the siege), the khagan ordered the assault to begin. His forces attacked along the full length of the land walls without respite for the whole of the day, again concentrating on the Lycus Valley; according to the *Chronicon Paschale*, 'he stationed a multitude of siege engines close to each other against that part which had been attacked by him, so that those in the city were compelled to station very many siege engines inside the wall,' to provide counter-battery fire.

Dusk did not bring an end to the struggle, 'and the combat continued on both sides throughout the night, without rest,' Theodore Syncellus recorded. Then, on the morning of Thursday 7 August, the front was broadened when the Slav fleet, carrying an infantry assault force, sailed towards the sea walls on the Golden Horn, assuming they had received a pre-arranged signal from the khagan for an amphibious assault against an unfortified beach. But the Byzantines had got wind of the Avar plan, and pre-empted the signal with one of their own. The assault force was lured into a massacre, the waters of the Golden Horn turning red with Slav blood.

It was the turning point. On the night of 7/8 August, the khagan gave the order to withdraw after setting fire to all the siege engines which he had deployed against the city. The flames lit up the evening sky and, according to Theodore Syncellus, 'For most of the following day, we could see neither the city nor the sea, because of widespread smoke.' By that point, the only Avars left in the vicinity of the city were a cavalry rearguard. After setting fire to the churches on the shore of the Golden Horn in a spiteful parting shot, this too disappeared.

The Avars never recovered from this debacle, and in the year following the siege, Heraclius triumphed at the Battle of Nineveh; the Sasanians, exhausted, deposed their shah (Khosrow being incarcerated in a cell for five days before being shot to death slowly with arrows) and sued for peace.

Heraclius personally restored the fragments of the True Cross to Jerusalem. He had brought the empire back from the brink of destruction. Having won the war, what he needed now to win the peace was time: to secure the frontiers; to rebuild the cities; to restore the economy; to heal the divisions over religious doctrine that roiled Byzantine society.

Time, however, had run out.

A cataclysm was about to fall on both Byzantine and Persian superpowers. While they had fought the last and greatest of their wars, the tribes of Arabia, hitherto entirely peripheral to global affairs, had been united under the banner of a new faith: Islam. The heirs to the Prophet Muhammad were about to change the world forever.

THE HIGH TIDE OF JIHAD

The Islamic storm burst in full force upon the Fertile Crescent in 636. The Sasanian field army was smashed at al-Qādisiyyah; reeling, the Persians abandoned Ctesiphon and pulled back to the Iranian plateau. That same year, the Byzantine field army was annihilated in the six-day Battle of Yarmouk. The Arabs then rolled up the major cities of Syria, taking Damascus, Aleppo and Antioch. The last to fall was Caesarea, besieged from December 640

The Yarmouk River near the el-Hammeh hot springs, above its point of junction with the Jordan River. The six-day battle fought in this region in 636 ended forever the imperial control over the Levant that had begun with Pompey the Great seven centuries earlier. With the annihilation of his field army, Emperor Heraclius had no choice but to pull his garrisons back in a fighting retreat into Anatolia to establish a new defence line behind the Taurus Mountains. (The Library of Congress)

A silver drachma of Yazdegerd III (r.632–51), the last shah of Sasanian Persia. While the Byzantines barely held on against the onslaught of the caliphate, the Sasanians were completely overrun. In the wake of their victory over the last Sasanian army at Nāhavand in 642, the Arabs roamed at will across the Iranian plateau. Yazdegerd III was finally run to ground at Merv and murdered, aged 27. (Noble Numismatics, https://www.noble.com.au/)

to May 641 by the innovative and ambitious Arab general Mu'āwiya, who deployed 72 siege engines against the walls. When the city fell, all 7,000 of the garrison, save those evacuated by sea, were executed, to set an example. Egypt was conquered by 'Amr b. al-'As, the last Byzantine troops being evacuated from Alexandria on 17 September 642. The Arabs pressed south down the Nile towards Nubia and continued their advance west along the Mediterranean shore towards Carthage, while to the east the last Sasanian army was wiped out at Nāhavand, opening up all Central Asia to Islam.

To the north, the Arabs took Samosata in early 641 and raided Armenia for the first time, seizing Bitlis. In another *razzia* (hostile raid) the following year, Habib b. Maslama plundered the entire region north of Lake Van, while Umayr b. Sad-al-Ansari led a raid into Cilicia and Cappadocia. On 6 October 642, the Arabs captured Dvin, slew 12,000 men, and seized 35,000 women and children for the slave markets of the east.

The king of Armenia, Theodore Rstuni, reached out to Constantinople for assistance. The *stratêgos* Procopios arrived with imperial troops to aid the Armenians, and in 643 he and Theodore made a deep raid into Mesopotamia as far as the Edessa–Aleppo highway, crushing the Arab detachments and plundering the entire region.

In 644, a Byzantine army repulsed the Arabs in Cilicia (probably the invasion by 'Abd Allāh b. Qais), then entered Mesopotamia, but failed to link up with an allied army commanded by David Zacharuni, prince of Armenia, who suffered a crushing defeat. According to Armenian sources, meanwhile, Procopios was deserted by the Armenians and was similarly routed.

The breakdown in the alliance was provoked by the Byzantine demand that the Armenians return to the canons of the Chalcedon Council and abandon their Monophysite faith. In accord with the Patriarch, the emperor issued a decree bidding the Armenians to unite ecclesiastically with Constantinople. Refusing to subordinate his church, and sensing which way the tide of war was turning, Theodore proceeded to Damascus, alone, to meet with Mu'āwiya and come to terms.

In 646, commanded by the eunuch *stratêgos* Manuel, an imperial army on board a fleet reportedly consisting of 300 ships arrived off Alexandria. Al-Hakam records that as soon as the fleet appeared, the Christians of Alexandria rebelled, helped the army to disembark, and massacred the entire garrison. But Manuel did not follow up his victory. Rather than march against Babylon-on-the-Nile, the main defensive centre of the enemy where complete confusion had now taken reign, Manuel plundered the Delta region, thus turning the local population against him and giving the Arabs the time needed to reassemble their scattered forces.

When they had recovered from the initial shock of this unexpected attack, the Arabs demanded the recall of 'Amr, the conqueror of Egypt, who was sent without delay. 'Amr rallied the defence and mobilized a strong force of 15,000 men, which, moreover, now had the (at least passive) support of the Coptic population.

Manuel advanced along the Nile as far as the town of Nikiu, where he was confronted by 'Amr. The imperial army initially had the advantage, but was ultimately outmanoeuvred and forced to retreat, its withdrawal degenerating into a rout with the Arabs in hot pursuit. The Byzantine force made a stand in Alexandria, but the besieging Arabs forced entry, either by direct assault or treachery. In either case, the Arabs surged into the streets of Alexandria, putting all to the sword, looting and burning. Manuel was slain in a bitterly fought clash in the heart of the city. The survivors fled

The city walls of Damascus, one of the wealthy municipalities in the Levant that Heraclius conceded to the jihad after the defeat at Yarmouk. It was not just Byzantine citizens who joined the exodus from Syria; many of the empire's Arab allies elected to pull back into Anatolia with the retreating imperial forces. (The Library of Congress)

Anatolia, 640–715

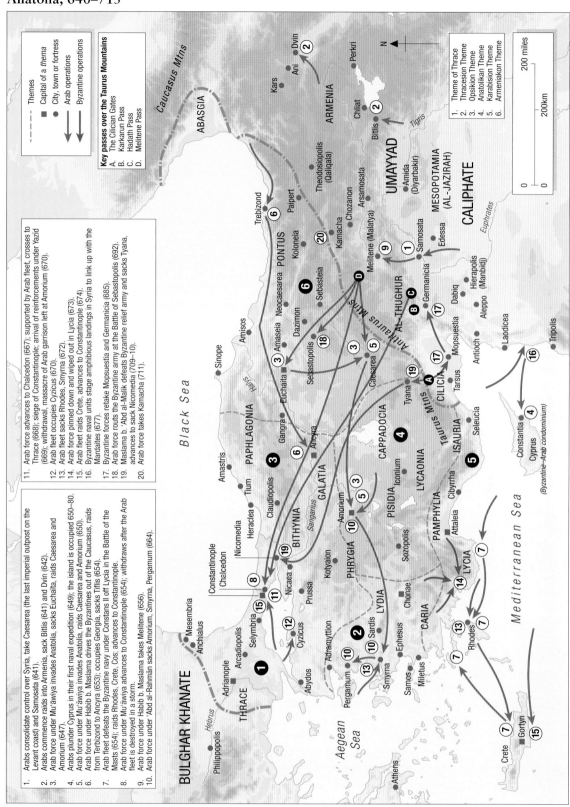

Themes
- – – – – Themes
- ■ Capital of a *thema*
- ● City, town or fortress
- → Arab operations
- → Byzantine operations

Key passes over the Taurus Mountains
- A. The Cilician Gates
- B. Karkarun Pass
- C. Hadath Pass
- D. Melitene Pass

1. Theme of Thrace
2. Thracesion Theme
3. Opsikion Theme
4. Anatolikan Theme
5. Karabison Theme
6. Armeniakon Theme

0 —— 200 miles
0 —— 200km

1. Arabs consolidate control over Syria, take Caesarea (the last imperial outpost on the Levant coast) and Samosata (641).
2. Arabs commence raids into Armenia, sack Bitlis (641) and Dvin (642).
3. Arab force under Mu'āwiya invades Anatolia, sacks Euchaita, raids Caesarea and Amorium (647).
4. Arabs plunder Cyprus in their first naval expedition (649); the island is occupied 650–80.
5. Arab force under Mu'āwiya invades Anatolia, raids Caesarea and Amorium (650).
6. Arab force under Habib b. Maslama drives the Byzantines out of the Caucasus, raids from Terbizond to Ancyra (653); occupies Georgia, sacks Tiflis (654).
7. Arab fleet defeats the Byzantine navy under Constans II off Lycia in the Battle of the Masts (654); raids Rhodes, Crete, Cos; advances to Constantinople.
8. Arab force under Mu'āwiya advances to Constantinople (654); withdraws after the Arab fleet is destroyed in a storm.
9. Arab force under Habib b. Maslama takes Melitene (656).
10. Arab force under 'Abd al-Rahman sacks Amorium, Smyrna, Pergamum (664).
11. Arab force advances to Chalcedon (667); supported by Arab fleet, crosses to Thrace (668); siege of Constantinople; arrival of reinforcements under Yazid (669); withdrawal, massacre of Arab garrison left at Amorium (670).
12. Arab fleet occupies Cyzicus (670).
13. Arab fleet sacks Rhodes, Smyrna (672).
14. Arab force pinned down and wiped out in Lycia (673).
15. Arab fleet raids Crete, advances to Constantinople (674).
16. Byzantine naval units stage amphibious landings in Syria to link up with the Mardaites (677).
17. Byzantine forces retake Mopsuestia and Germanicia (685).
18. Arab force routs the Byzantine army at the Battle of Sebastopolis (692).
19. Maslama b. 'Abd al-Malik defeats Byzantine relief army and sacks Tyana, advances to sack Nicomedia (709–10).
20. Arab force takes Kamacha (711).

to the ships of the imperial fleet, which set sail from the harbour in haste. It was with great difficulty that 'Amr succeeded in bringing a halt to the destruction, but only after a large section of the city, including the church of St Mark, had been consumed by the flames. 'Amr subsequently tore down the walls of Alexandria, and imposed a heavy tax on the rebellious inhabitants.

In 647, Mu'āwiya led a powerful force into Cappadocia, 'leaving a trail of destruction behind him,' one account records. He took Euchaïta when its populace 'were scattered over the countryside, harvesting the crops and working in the vineyards … The Arabs found the gates of the unhappy city open.' Michael the Syrian states the raiders 'enslaved the entire population, men and women, boys and girls. They committed a great orgy in this unfortunate city, fornicating wickedly inside the churches.' After leaving Euchaïta 'ravaged and deserted', Mu'āwiya advanced to Caesarea, then proceeded to Amorium, where he was repulsed. He retraced his steps to Caesarea, which finally agreed to pay tribute in order to raise the siege. In Cilicia, he destroyed all fortifications between Antioch and Tarsus that had been abandoned by the imperial forces before his army returned to caliphal territory, burdened with much loot.

Up to this point, Arab expansion had proceeded exclusively on land. Mu'āwiya urged *amir al-mu'minin* ('leader of the faithful') 'Umar b. al-Khattāb to support the armies of the believers with a permanent naval force in the Mediterranean (the *al-bahr al-rūm*, as the Arabs called it, 'the Sea of the Romans'), without which the newly won territories would always be vulnerable. He cited the raids by imperial marines launched from the island of Arwad, so near the Syrian shore he could hear 'the barking of the Byzantines' dogs and the crow of their cock'. 'Umar solicited the opinion of 'Amr b. al-'As, the governor of Egypt, on the subject. His reply described the open water as an environment that 'terrifies the senses', where 'the faculties become numb, and the calamities augment'. A ship was 'a huge creature floating on the sea, on which men seemed to be diminutive things … Those inside it are like worms in a log. If it inclines to one side, they are drowned. If it escapes, they are confounded.' On receiving this perspective, 'Umar denied Mu'āwiya authority to initiate a naval component of the jihad; 'Let the sea remain a barrier between us and the enemy. By Allah I will not set a true believer upon it.'

Mu'āwiya's strategic insight had to simmer until five years after 'Umar was succeeded by the more worldly 'Uthmān b. Affan. The new *amir al-mu'minin* was prepared to endorse a naval campaign, provided it was comprised exclusively of volunteers. In 649, having ordered Habib b. Maslama to lead a raid into Isauria that would draw imperial attention, Mu'āwiya outfitted a fleet under the command of Abd Allāh b. Qais, supported by another fleet sent by 'Abd Allāh b. Abi Sarh from Egypt. This force overran Cyprus; the populace fled to their fortified strongholds which, in the words of Michael the Syrian, 'became their cemeteries. The sword of Hagar fell upon them and a very great multitude were killed.' Constantia, the island's capital, was 'besieged and then destroyed', the Arabs 'filling it with blood and thoroughly looting it'. The following year, another of Mu'āwiya's

This gold solidus emphasizes the intent of Emperor Heraclius (r.610–41) to be succeeded by his young son from his first marriage, Constantine. When Heraclius died, this line of succession did play out, but Constantine III was already mortally ill and died in turn just three months later. Heraclius's second wife then attempted to raise her son, Heraclonas, to the throne, only for the army to depose and mutilate both her and Heraclonas in favour of Constantine's son, Constans II. The general responsible, Valentine, married his daughter to Constans but then went too far when he attempted to usurp the throne himself and wound up being lynched by the enraged citizens of Constantinople. (Noble Numismatics, https://www.noble.com.au/)

This gold solidus of Constans II (r. 641–68) features his portrait along with that of his eldest son and eventual successor Constantine IV (r.668–85) on the obverse, with his two younger sons – Heraclius (left) and Tiberius (right) – on the reverse. Constans was not quite 11 years old when he became sole ruler on 9 November 641. His major contribution to the survival of Byzantine civilization was his reorganization of the army and the remaining territories into the decentralized thematic system that embedded the military into the communities it defended and enabled immediate local response to the threat of invasion. (Noble Numismatics, https://www. noble.com.au/)

subordinates, Abū'l-A'war, who had fought at Yarmouk, again plundered Cyprus, this time establishing a garrison that would remain in occupation of the island for three decades until Mu'āwiya's son Yazīd withdrew them in 680.

Meanwhile, Mu'āwiya divided his forces, sending one division north under Habib b. Maslama into Armenia. It was October when they set out, late in the campaign season, especially for mountain country, and Michael the Syrian records that when this force entered the highlands, 'they found the land filled with snow. Employing a ruse, they brought in oxen which they led before them to clear the road. In this way, they advanced without being impeded by the snow. The Armenians, who had not foreseen this, were attacked when they did not expect it. The [Arabs] embarked on devastation and pillage. They took captive the population, set fire to the villages and returned to their country joyfully.'

The main army, under the personal command of Mu'āwiya, advanced on Caesarea in Cappadocia, where 'they found the villages full of men and animals and seized them. After collecting booty from the whole country, Mu'āwiya attacked the town. He fought against it for ten days,' then, having 'totally devastated the whole province', he moved on. A few days later, the Arabs returned to Caesarea. 'They fought against it for many days.' With no relief in sight, the citizenry 'agreed to negotiate for their lives', offering tribute in exchange for a halt to the siege. The Arabs 'took everything they wanted' and moved on to Amorium. After surrounding it and 'realizing that it was impregnable', they offered to spare the lives of the inhabitants if they surrendered on terms. Rebuffed, Mu'āwiya sent his troops to ravage the countryside; 'they plundered gold, silver, riches like dust, and returned to their country'.

These vignettes are significant in what they reveal about the warfare of the period. Motivated by opportunities for plunder, Arab armies were fast moving and devastating in open country, but their mobility came at the expense of a siege train, obliging them to leave fortified urban centres unsubdued in their wake.

In 651, Constans II negotiated a two-year peace treaty with Mu'āwiya. But after the final Sasanian collapse eliminated any threat from that quarter, Mu'āwiya began preparations for the definitive campaign against the Byzantine Empire. Sebeos relates, 'he commanded his troops to conduct war by sea and land in order to efface from the Earth that kingdom as well', for, as Mu'āwiya recognized, 'tighten the noose around Constantinople and the other nations will follow'.

The war would be carried forward on multiple fronts. In 653, Mu'āwiya dispatched an Arab army led by Habib b. Maslama to Armenia, where it linked up with Theodore, drove the Byzantines out of the Caucasus, and penetrated as far as Trebizond and Ancyra. In 654, Theodosiopolis (Erzurum) fell, Georgia was plundered, and Tiflis was occupied, Habib b. Maslama offering its citizens the standard terms: 'If you submit [to God] and perform the prayer and pay *zakat*, then [you are] our brothers in religion and our clients. Whosoever turns away from God and His prophets and His books and His party, we summon you to war without distinction; God does not love traitors.'

In 654, the Arab field army advanced rapidly through Byzantine territory, encountering no effective resistance; according to Sebeos, as Muʿāwiya 'penetrated the whole land, all the inhabitants of the country submitted to him, those on the coast and in the mountains and on the plains'. Muʿāwiya had also made extensive preparations for a massive naval campaign, ordering the construction of 300 transport ships and 5,000 light warships, each fitted out with only one hundred men 'for the sake of speed', Sebeos records, 'so that they might rapidly dart to and fro over the waves of the sea around the very large ships'.

An Arab fleet under the command of Abū'l-Aʿwar confronted the Byzantine navy under the personal command of Constans off the coast of Lycia. What the Arabs called the Battle of the Masts (Dhāt al-Sawārī) took place, in the words of Sebeos, 'on a sea so violent it was said that dense spray ascended among the ships like dust from dry land and that the sea was dyed with blood'. It was a complete triumph for the Arabs. The *Continuatio Isidoriana Hispana* relates that Constans had 'gathered over a thousand boats but was unlucky in the fight and barely managed to escape with a handful of men'. Theophanes describes Constans only managing to escape the disaster by dressing one of his subordinates in regal attire as a decoy before he 'abandoned all his men and sailed away to Constantinople', leaving 23,000 corpses to wash ashore behind him.

In the wake of this rout, the Arab fleet passed unhindered into the Aegean, where Abū'l-Aʿwar took Crete, Rhodes, and Cos before entering the Dardanelles en route to linking up with the army at Chalcedon. Muʿāwiya was now gazing across the Bosporus at Constantinople itself when a second fleet arrived from Alexandria under ʿAbd Allāh b. Abi Sarh with reinforcements and, critically, siege engines. According to Sebeos, 'they had stowed on board the ships mangonels, and machines to throw fire, and machines to hurl stones, archers and slingers, so that when they reached the walls of the city they might easily descend from the top of the towers and break into the city'. Muʿāwiya 'ordered the ships to be deployed in lines and to attack'. With this one last dagger thrust at its exposed heart, the empire would surely fall. Cornered, Constans is reported to have 'lifted the crown from his head, stripped off his purple [robes] ... put on sackcloth, sat on ashes, and ordered a fast be proclaimed', throwing the destiny of his line to the chance of divine intervention.

And fate took a hand. As Sebeos recorded:

When they were about two stades' distance from the dry land, then one could see the awesome power of the Lord. For the Lord looked down from heaven with the violence of a fierce wind, and there arose a storm, a great

This miniature from the 16th-century *Siyer-i Nebi*, a Turkish epic about the life of Muhammad written by Mustafa, son of Yusuf of Erzurum, depicts Muhammad's widow, ʿĀ'ishah, battling her erstwhile son-in-law Alī b. Abi Talib in the Battle of the Camel, so called because ʿĀ'ishah led her army in person from camelback in an armoured *howdah* that 'bristled like a porcupine' from all the arrow hits it took. The battle only ended when the camel was hamstrung and brought down. ʿĀ'ishah, her arm pinioned by an arrow, was taken prisoner. (Universal Images Group/Art Resource, NY)

tempest, and the sea was stirred up from the depths below. Its waves piled up high like the summits of very high mountains … On that day by his upraised arm God saved the city through the prayers of the pious king Constans.

The Arab fleet was wrecked. Bereft of naval support, Muʿāwiya elected not to proceed with the siege and withdrew to Syria. Heartened, the Byzantines defeated the Arab army stationed in Cappadocia and forced it to evacuate imperial territory. The following year, the Byzantine army led by Maurianos launched a counterattack in Armenia. The Arabs were repulsed, and 'beset by snow' were obliged to retreat south.

Natural forces had saved the empire; Arab infighting would now endow it with a critical five-year breathing space. In 656, Muʿāwiya ordered Habib b. Maslama to take Melitene. An Arab garrison was established there and the city became a jumping-off point for many raids into Asia Minor. But that same year, ʿUthmān b. Affan was assassinated. Alī b. Abi Talib succeeded him as *amir al-muʾminin*, but failed to stamp his authority over the ever-expanding and increasingly diverse *Dar-al-Islam* (the territories under Muslim rule). Old grudges and new rivalries within Islam erupted in the first Muslim civil war (*fitna*). 'The blood of the slaughter of immense multitudes flowed thickly among the armies of Ishmael', the *Armenian History* records: 'Warfare afflicted them as they engaged in mutual carnage.' Alī defeated ʿĀʾishah, widow of the Prophet Muhammad, in the Battle of the Camel, but was faced down by Muʿāwiya in the 657 Battle of Siffin. The assassination of Alī allowed for Muʿāwiya to assume control in 661 – dubbed the 'year of coming together' (*ʿam al-jamaʾa*) in Muslim tradition – which ushered in two decades of relative stability. Muʿāwiya formalized authority in his person as caliph, a title intended to be hereditary within his Umayyad clan.

Constans had taken advantage of the Arab internecine strife by striking a truce with Muʿāwiya in 659. The Armenians drifted back into the imperial sphere of influence, while Constans campaigned successfully in Macedonia, resettling numerous Slavs in Anatolia. But after he ordered the execution of his brother, Theodosius, on charges of treason, he was repudiated by the people of Constantinople, who cursed him as 'Cain' whenever he appeared in public. Accordingly, he took the unprecedented step of abandoning the city in 662, travelling via Thessalonica to Athens, then crossing to Italy, where he campaigned against the Lombards and visited Rome before settling in Syracuse. He sent for his wife and children, but the Senate refused to countenance their relocation.

Muʿāwiya kept the peace until he was rid of Ali and had subdued Iraq in 661. The Arab campaigns against the empire resumed in 662; Theophanes records their incursion 'taking many prisoners and devastating many places'. This is confirmed by al-Ṭabarī, who notes that Arab raiders under Busr b. Abī Arṭāt killed several 'patricians' (*batariqah*). These raids would continue on an almost annual basis; sensing weakness, Arab forces increasingly dared to winter in Asia Minor. Since large parts of the imperial

Constantine IV (668–85) is depicted in a warrior's pose on the obverse of this gold solidus, with his brothers Heraclius and Tiberius on the reverse. He ascended to the throne when his father Constans II was fatally attacked in his bath in Syracuse by his attendant Andreas. The teenage Constantine had to act fast to crush the insurgency in Sicily, then confront the onset of a massive Arab invasion that was striking at the heart of his empire. He proved equal to the challenge, and emerged as a truly formidable emperor. (Noble Numismatics, https://www.noble.com.au/)

army had moved west with Constans II, those forces that remained in Asia Minor lacked the strength to meet the Arabs in open battle. The imperial presence contracted to the major cities and other strategic chokepoints.

Raids in 662 and 663 were preparatory for the significant campaign of 'Abd al-Rahmān b. Khālid b. al-Walīd, son of the great conqueror, who crossed the Taurus in 664 and traversed the length of Anatolia to the Aegean; according to the *Maronite Chronicle*, Amorium surrendered and Pessinus, Cius, Pergamum, and Smyrna were taken. He wintered on imperial territory over 665 before returning to Hims in 666. There he was poisoned by his Christian physician b. Uthāl on the instigation of Mu'āwiya, who feared the emergence of a rival.

The following year, Saborius, the Magister Militum per Armeniam who had rebelled against Constans II, entered into negotiations with Mu'āwiya. However, by the time Arab troops commanded by Faḍālah b. 'Ubayd al-Ansārī arrived at Melitene to follow up on this opportunity, Saborius was already dead (killed neither in battle nor by intrigue, but by his horse, which reared up as he passed through a narrow gate and fractured his skull), and the revolt had been put down by the *patricius* Nicephorus. Left to his own devices, Faḍālah requested reinforcements; Mu'āwiya sent a powerful force led by veteran commanders, all of them Companions of the Prophet: 'Abd Allāh b. 'Abbās, paternal cousin of the Prophet and ancestor of the Abbasids; 'Abd Allāh b. 'Umar, son of the second *amir al-mu'minin* and one of the most important transmitters of Hadith; 'Abd Allāh b. al-Zubayr, son of a sister of the Prophet's wife 'Ā'ishah and grandson of Abū Bakr; and Abū Ayyūb al-Ansārī, who had hosted the Prophet during his residence in Medina.

The joint Arab force wintered in Chalcedon in 667/68. The army crossed over to Thrace and laid siege to Constantinople the following year, supported by a fleet. Two major naval campaigns are mentioned by al-Ṭabarī, of the Egyptians and the people of Medina in 668–69, and of the Syrian and Egyptian fleets in the following year. The extent of the total mobilization for this campaign is reflected in papyrus records which mention sailors recruited from as far afield as Apollonos Ano (Edfu) – located a thousand kilometres up the Nile – to serve in the Egyptian naval squadron that participated in the expedition. The effect was to isolate Constantinople from the outside world. The Patriarch Thomas II apologized to Pope Vitalian for his being unable to communicate 'because, as you know, of the protracted incursions of the impious Saracens and their presence throughout the two years' since he had taken office in 667.

At this moment of deepening peril, the Byzantine state was plunged into further crisis on 15 July 668. As Constans II was reclining in his bath, his attendant, Andreas, son of a high-ranking judge in Constantinople, 'so covered his head with soapsuds that he was unable to open his eyes. Then he took a silver bucket, which he had placed in front of the king, and brought it crashing down on his head, fracturing his skull.' In the wake of this assassination the Magister Militum Praesentalis, an Armenian named Mžež Gnuni, was acclaimed emperor Mizizios at Syracuse.

This mosaic from the Basilica of Sant'Apollinare in Classe, depicting Emperor Constantine IV granting privileges to the Church of Ravenna, commemorates one of the last formal expressions of Byzantine authority in the city prior to the final collapse of imperial control. The emperor here is accompanied by his two brothers, Tiberius and Heraclius. In 669, rebel troops marched to Chrysopolis and demanded that Constantine share the throne with his brothers as co-emperors. Constantine crushed the revolt, and had his brothers' noses slit to remove them from any future consideration as rivals or alternatives. (akg-images/Cameraphoto)

In the absence of the court, the administration of Constantinople had devolved upon a regency council headed by the patrician Theodore of Koloneia and the *cubicularios* Andrew. They acclaimed one of Constans' three sons as emperor Constantine IV.

Though their world appeared to be falling apart, the Byzantines remained defiant. Far from seeking terms, Constantine IV dispatched Andrew the *cubicularios* to Muʿāwiya to deliver the message: 'we shall have recourse to God, who has more power than you to defend the Romans, and we shall place our hope in Him'.

This faith was not misplaced, as the Arab camp was rife with disease. Yazīd, the son of Muʿāwiya, who was being groomed for the succession, is said to have composed the following verse upon hearing about the suffering of the Arab army:

> When I lie on carpets drinking a morning draught in Dayr Murrān with Umm Kulthūm
> What do I care about troops suffering from fever and smallpox?

The Edirne Gate (the Byzantine Gate of Charisius) stands at the peak of the sixth hill of Constantinople and is thus at the highest point in the old city, 12m above sea level. It was through this gate that the Ottoman Sultan Mehmet II made his triumphal entry into Constantinople on 29 May 1453. (Author's collection)

Informed of this poem, Muʿāwiya raged, 'I swear by God, you shall enter Byzantine territory, and let what befell them befall you!' He dispatched his son at the head of reinforcements (100,000 strong, according to the *Continuatio Byzantia-Arabica*, and including Husayn b. Alī) intended to succour the Arab troops – hence the name of the 'succouring expedition' (*ghazwah al-rādifah*) – and consummate the conquest of Constantinople.

According to Arab tradition, two tents had been put up in Constantinople next to the city wall. One of them resounded with tambourines, drums, and flutes whenever the Arabs were attacking, while the other responded in a similar way to every Roman charge. The former belonged to the daughter of the emperor, the latter to the daughter of Jabalah b. al-Ayham, the last Ghassanid ruler exiled to Byzantium. Yazīd, determined to please the Ghassanid princess, defeated the Byzantines before the walls, drove them back into the city, and hammered one of the great gates with an iron club until it broke in two.

A more grounded appraisal of the siege, incorporating the tactical initiatives undertaken by the two sides, occurs in the *Maronite Chronicle*:

> While they were encamped in Thrace, the Arabs scattered for the purpose of plunder, leaving their hirelings and their sons to pasture the cattle and to snatch anything that should come their way. When those who were standing on the wall saw this, they went out and fell upon them and killed a great many young men and hirelings and some of the Arabs too. Then they snatched up the booty and went in to the City. The next day, all the young men of the City grouped together, along with some of those who had come in to take refuge there and a few of the Romans and said, 'Let us make a sortie against them.' But Constantine told them, 'Do not make a sortie. It is not as if you had engaged in a battle and won. All you have done is a bit of common

thieving.' But they refused to listen to him. Instead, a large number of people went out armed, carrying banners and streamers on high as is the Roman custom. As soon as they had gone out, all the gates were closed. The King had a tent erected on the wall, where he sat watching. The Saracens drew them after them, retreating a good long way away from the wall, so that they would not be able to escape quickly when put to flight. So they went out and squatted in tribal formation. When the others reached them, they leapt to their feet and cried out in the way of their language, 'God is great!' Immediately the others turned tail in flight, chased by the Saracens, who fell on them, killing and making captives right up to the point where they came within range of the catapults on the wall. In his fury with them Constantine was barely willing to open the gates for them. Many of them fell and others were wounded by arrows.

Such successes notwithstanding, conditions in the Arab camp were becoming untenable, and it was this factor that forced a premature end to the campaign. According to the *Continuatio Isidoriana Hispana*, 'When they had carried on the siege throughout the spring season and could no longer bear the hardships of hunger and pestilence, they abandoned the city.' Even after this setback, however, the Arabs retained the tactical initiative as they 'seized many towns' throughout their retreat through Anatolia and returned to Damascus 'laden with booty'. In fact, the Arab withdrawal may have been owed more to Byzantine gold than active resistance; the *Chronicle of 1234* reports the Arabs 'took captives and plundered, and generally did as they wanted. Under the pressure of this aggression the Romans offered them gifts; the Arabs made peace and went back to their country.' One of the towns taken was Amorium, where the Arabs left a garrison of 5,000 men before departing for Syria. That winter, however, the *cubicularios* Andrew stormed the city in a daring night assault; covered by a blizzard, his men used stakes to scale the wall and once inside massacred the entire garrison.

The oldest and greatest of Constantinople's gates, the Golden Gate, located at the southern end of the land walls, was originally a triumphal arch, erected in honour of Emperor Theodosius I towards the end of the 4th century, that was later integrated into the city's defences. It marked the end of the major trans-Balkans highway, the Via Egnatia, and the beginning of Constantinople's main street, the Mese. (Author's collection)

Both sides claimed victory, both ascribing it to their respective faiths. In a liturgy on 25 June, the Patriarch of Constantinople praised 'the help provided contrary to reason and beyond any hope by the great God and our Saviour Jesus Christ … against the godless Saracens who were besieging our imperial city by land and sea'. After his return from Constantinople, where he had done enough to be hailed as the *fatā al-Arab* (young champion of the Arabs), Yazīd led the pilgrimage to Mecca, while the following year the hajj was led by Mu'āwiya himself, who used this occasion to declare Yazīd as heir apparent and to secure the support of the key figures of the *ummah* for this controversial decision. The three Companions who survived the campaign against Constantinople – b. 'Abbās, b. 'Umar, and b. al-Zubayr – opposed Mu'āwiya's choice; but Yazīd's campaign must have been considered successful enough to lend legitimacy to Mu'āwiya's attempt to establish the dynastic principle of succession in the caliphate.

Meanwhile, loyalist imperial troops from Italy and the Exarchate of Africa suppressed the revolt in Sicily, executed Mizizios, and sent his severed head to Constantinople. This

The inner wall of Constantinople boasted no fewer than 96 towers. Most were square, but some were hexagonal, heptagonal, or octagonal. They were spaced between 53.3m and 55.1m apart, from 17.3m to 18.3m high with a projection of 5.5m to 10.3m. Many towers retain their original Greek inscriptions commemorating repairs and reconstruction sponsored by the emperors over the course of Byzantine history, including Leo IV, Constantine VI, Basil II, John VIII, and the Empress Irene. The seventh tower of the inner wall bears the names of Leo III and Constantine V with the legend, 'Oh Christ, God, preserve thy city undisturbed and free from war. Conquer the wrath of our enemies.' (Author's collection)

did little to resolve the empire's vulnerability to Arab incursions, by land, or, increasingly, by sea. In the passage immediately following its description of the fall of Mizizios, the *Liber Pontificalis* reports:

> Afterwards the Saracens came to Sicily, occupied Syracuse, and caused much slaughter among the people who had fled to the walled towns and the hills. They returned to Alexandria taking with them enormous booty and the bronze which had been brought there by sea from Rome.

The frontier in Asia Minor was wide open to assault. In 670, Busr b. Abī Arṭāt campaigned in summer, Sufyān b. 'Awf al-Azdī in winter. Faḍālah b. 'Ubayd al-Ansārī entered the Sea of Marmara at the head of another fleet and wintered at Cyzicus. In 671, Muhammad b. 'Abd al-Rahmān led the summer campaign. In 672, Sufyān led the summer campaign, while the Arab fleet ravaged the shores of Anatolia, wintering on imperial territory in three detachments. One squadron, led by Muhammad b. 'Abd al-Rahmān, wintered at Smyrna; a second, under Junāda b. Abī Umayya al-Azdī, seized Tarsus in Cilicia, then went on to conquer Rhodes; while a third, led by 'Abd Allāh b. Qais, wintered in Lycia. Byzantine patricians Florus, Petronas, and Cyprianus converged their forces on this incursion and the Arabs were crushed, losing 30,000 dead in the ensuing engagement.

To hinder the operations of the Egyptian fleet, in 673 the Byzantines landed troops at al-Burullus in the Nile Delta. According to al-Kindī, the governor of Egypt Maslama b. Mukhallad dispatched a force to oppose this incursion and a great battle ensued in which many Arabs were slain, among whom were some of the outstanding military leaders of Egypt.

Reinforced by another fleet (probably the Egyptian, led by 'Abd al-Rahmān b. al-Hakam), an Arab armada under the command of Junāda sailed through the Hellespont in April 674 and appeared under the walls of Constantinople. In the Arab tradition, Sufyān b. 'Awf al-Azdī rode at the head of 3,000 cavalry to the city, where he engaged in the following dialogue:

[Sufyān] raided with us as far as the Golden Gate, so that the people of Constantinople were alarmed and rang the bells. They came to meet us and said:

'What do you want, o troop of Arabs? Why did you come?'

'We have come to destroy this city of unbelief, and God will destroy it by our hands.'

'We do not know whether your plan is wrong, or the [Qur'an] lied, or you have arrived before the preordained time. By God, we know that the city will be conquered one day, but we do not think that the time is now.'

'All day long,' from April to September, according to Theophanes, 'from dawn to dusk there was combat from the outworks of the Golden Gate to the Cyclobion; both sides were thrusting and counter-thrusting.' But the walls held, and the Arabs 'were disgraced, expending a host of warlike men'. The Byzantines were able to maintain the edge at sea thanks to a new terror weapon. Theophanes records that Constantine IV 'built large biremes bearing cauldrons of fire and dromons equipped with siphons and ordered them to be stationed at the Proclianesian harbour of Constantinople'. Agapius maintains the Arab fleet 'was completely burned. That year the [Byzantines] were favoured with victory. They were the first to make use of [Greek] fire, and they usually made use of it [thereafter].' The surviving vessels 'retreated in great distress,' Theophanes records. As the fleet withdrew to home waters, 'it was overtaken by a tempestuous winter storm near Syllaion,' in Pamphylia, on the southern coast of Anatolia, where it was 'completely destroyed'.

However, the Arabs were far from giving up on their efforts to wrest control of the sea lanes from Constantinople. Another Arab fleet, under Faḍālah and 'Abd Allāh b. Qais, wintered in Crete with the expectation of resuming operations in the Aegean the following year. And in the summer of 675 the incursions into Anatolia resumed, this one being led by Junāda b. Abī Umayya al-Azdī, who had known the *amir al-mu'minin* Abū Bakr and 'Umar and the scholar Mu'adh b. Jabal and was accounted a reliable chronicler of Hadith, the traditions of earliest Islam. But that year the Byzantines counterattacked, landing on the Syrian coast just south of Bāniyās, where the governor of Ḥimṣ 'Abd Allāh b. Qurṭ al-Thumālī al-Azdī was killed. Imperial forces also scored some signal victories in Asia Minor; 'Abd Allāh b. Qais, a Companion of the Prophet, was killed during the course of the 676/77 winter campaign, while the 677/78 winter campaign culminated in the defeat and death of Yazīd b. Shajarah.

Still the Arabs kept coming. In 679, forces led by Ṣafwān b. al-Mu'aṭṭal al-Sulamī and Umayr b. al-Hubab seized the important fortress of Camach. In the same year, 'Amr b. Murra al-Jahunī (an old fighter who Mu'āwiya had dubbed 'the lion of Juhayna') invaded and wintered in Byzantine territory. Significantly, b. Wāḍih al-Yaqūbī records, 'In that year there was no [campaign] by sea', but in 680, Malik b. 'Abd Allāh invaded imperial territory, reaching as far as Isauria in south-eastern Asia Minor.

These incursions were becoming an endemic feature of life for the households caught up in this relentless drumbeat

The Gate of St Romanus, between towers 65 and 66, is the second largest behind the Golden Gate. The stretch of walls between this gate and the Gate of Charisius was called the *mesoteichion*, the most vulnerable point in the defence line, where the walls descend into the Lycus Valley. (Author's collection)

of war. An account from a collection of miracles ascribed to St Theodore and associated with the town of Euchaïta in north-central Asia Minor describes in detail how the population took to their fortified acropolis behind the town 'when the yearly raid of the Saracens came', returning only after the enemy had departed with its booty.

The empire was being stretched to its limit. When the Slavs laid siege to Thessaloniki in 676, the emperor could spare no more than ten ships for its defence the following year, the rest of the fleet being 'busy with another war'. The primary commitment of 677 was a naval expedition to land troops on the coast of Syria. These linked up with the Mardaites (from the Aramaic *Maridaye*, 'the rebellious ones'), the indigenous residents of the Mt Amanus region around Antioch, described by a near contemporary as 'the armed men who from olden times had practiced banditry in the mountains of Lebanon'. As their ranks swelled with refugees and runaway slaves, they became more aggressive, raiding as far afield as Galilee.

This metastasizing threat, so close to the centre of Umayyad power in Damascus, was enough to tip the balance of the war. A 30-year truce was concluded between the caliphate and the empire, formalized by oaths between Constantine IV and Yazīd, who had succeeded his father Muʿāwiya as caliph upon the latter's death in 680 and needed to focus on consolidating his dynastic inheritance of power. Under the agreed terms, the Arabs were to make an annual payment of 3,000 pounds of gold, 50 hostages, and 50 horses of fine breed. Yazīd also ordered the immediate withdrawal of the Arab garrisons from Rhodes and Cyprus.

The empire, pushed to the brink, had won a reprieve. This had only been possible through its reinvention as a garrison state dedicated exclusively to conditions of total war, in which the ordinary rhythms of life were suspended. The *sacra* of Constantine IV to the Pope, dated 12 August 678, though expressing hope the desired reconciliation of the churches 'will put an end to the turmoil that is being inflicted on us by the tribes', repeatedly stressed the impossibility of convoking a general council because 'the times do not allow it'. It took another two years for the strategic situation to stabilize to the point where the emperor was finally able to host a delegation from the Curia to the Sixth Ecumenical Council, which reasserted orthodoxy and declared the monothelite sect heretical. In his statement to the opening session on 10 September 680, he made a point of noting the delegates convened under the shadow of an existential crisis: 'Even though Our Serenity is ceaselessly afflicted by military and political anxieties, nevertheless we place all the affairs of our Christ-loving state second to our most Christian faith, which in war is a defender both of ourselves and of our Christ-loving armies.' A late-7th-century text known as the *Trophies of Damascus* emphasizes this point: 'This is the most remarkable, that the church, having fought, remained invincible

A gold solidus of Emperor Justinian II (r.685–95, 705–11). Inheriting the throne aged just 16, Justinian was ambitious and aggressive, taking the fight to the Umayyad enemy and sponsoring far-reaching building and population transfer policies (such as resettling large numbers of Slavs in Anatolia). His fate of being deposed twice was symptomatic of an era where the Byzantine state, beset by external enemies, descended into internal anarchy, when six emperors took power and then lost it within 21 years. (Noble Numismatics, https://www.noble.com.au/)

The immense scale of the Temple of Bacchus in Baalbek, contemporary Lebanon, speaks to the significant imprint of Greco-Roman culture in the region. The final manifestation of this identity, however, would take the form of an insurgency of runaway slaves and escaped prisoners of war that centred on the surrounding mountain country and metastasized to the point where it was considered an existential threat by the Umayyad caliphs. These people were dubbed the Jarajima by their enemies; the Byzantines called them the Mardaites. Neutralizing them became a priority for the caliphs in order to secure the Umayyad heartland. (Author's collection)

and indestructible, and while all struck it, the foundation remained unmoved. While the head and the empire stood firm, the whole body could be renewed.'

Byzantine recovery was aided by a fresh round of bloodletting within the caliphate. When Husayn b. Alī, son of the fourth *amir al-mu'minin*, was invited by sympathizers in Iraq to overthrow the Umayyads and claim his inheritance, he was killed with his small company en route to Kufa at the Battle of Karbala in October 680. This encounter institutionalized the division between orthodox Muslims (the Sunni) and the party of Alī (the Shi'a). In 683, a second *fitna* erupted in Mecca when 'Abd Allāh b. al-Zubayr repudiated Yazīd in an insulting sermon ('Yazīd of drink, Yazīd of whores … Yazīd of apes, Yazīd of dogs'). Yazīd dispatched an army to the Hejaz that sacked Medina and laid siege to Mecca, but with the Kaabah in flames, Yazīd died on 12 November 683, and the Umayyad onslaught

This enormous aqueduct, which brought water to Carthage from the springs of Zahouan and Djouar in Tunisia 140km (88 miles) away, was constructed early in the 2nd century AD by the Roman emperors Hadrian and Septimius Severus. The Arab subjugation of North Africa (Ifriqiyah) was much more protracted than the lightning conquest of the Levant, largely because of fierce resistance from the indigenous Berber tribes. It was not until 698 that a third Muslim invasion finally seized Carthage, expelling its citizens and razing its walls. In the spring of 710, Arab forces took the city of Tangier, completing the conquest of Ifriqiyah. (The Library of Congress)

A gold solidus of Leontius (r.695–98). Afraid of being blamed for the failure to retake Carthage from Arab control in 697, some Byzantine naval officers revolted and proclaimed as emperor Apsimar, the *droungarios* of the Kibyrrhaioton Theme. Apsimar sailed to Constantinople, and took the throne with the regnal name Tiberius III. Justinian II subsequently had Leontius executed. (Noble Numismatics, https://www.noble.com.au/)

ground to a halt. The designated heir, Mu'āwiya II, followed his father to the grave just months later, and the succession passed to Marwān b. al-Hakam, then to his son 'Abd al-Malik b. al-Marwān in April 685.

Convulsed with the internal strife at its core, the caliphate now struggled to retain control over its periphery. The Armenians seized this opportunity to throw off the yoke of Arab hegemony, while in Ifriqiyah, the caliphal campaign to take Carthage culminated in the defeat and death of Uqba b. Nāfi in 683 at the hands of the Byzantines and their Berber allies. In 684, the Byzantines occupied Ascalon and Caesarea on the coast of Palestine; both cities were pillaged and suffered considerable destruction. The following year, imperial forces took Mopsuestia and Germanicia, forcing the Arab inhabitants to migrate; Byzantine armies advanced as far as Melitene, and the Mardaites rose up in arms again. Beset by famine in addition to struggling to put down the defiance of al-Zubayr in Mecca, 'Abd al-Malik was in no position to countenance a protracted struggle with the empire. In 685, he requested a renewal of the peace treaty signed by Yazīd on even more generous terms for Constantinople. He sent an embassy to the young new emperor, Justinian II, offering 1,000 gold bezants, a slave, and a fine horse for every day of the year. It was also agreed the empire and caliphate would share the income from Cyprus and Armenia. In return, around 12,000 Mardaites were relocated to regions of Anatolia and Greece that remained under imperial authority. Although they would serve as rowers and marines in the Byzantine navy for several centuries, to Theophanes this arrangement amounted to 'mutilating the Roman state', for all the cities in the heights along the Taurus Mountains, 'which are now inhabited by the Arabs, had grown weak and depopulated from the Mardaites' attacks'. After they were transplanted, the caliphate was able to consolidate its strength along the frontier, and the empire 'suffered all sorts of evils at the hands of the Arabs up until the present day'.

With pressure on the eastern front reduced, Justinian II was free to campaign in the Balkans, where he pushed through to Thessaloniki, resettling many Slavs in Anatolia, large numbers of whom were drafted into the Opsikion Theme and a new mobile field army. Justinian II also personally led initiatives to restore imperial authority in Armenia.

The second *fitna* ended in 692 when 'Abd al-Malik dispatched al-Hajjaj b. Yusuf to suppress his rival in the Hejaz. Umayyad authority was graphically reasserted when, after the fall of Mecca, al-Zubayr's head was dispatched to Damascus while his decapitated corpse was crucified upside down outside the main gate to the city. With this internecine strife settled, the Arabs were again free to focus on the common enemy in Constantinople. Seizing on an attempt by Justinian II to forcibly resettle the population of Cyprus to Anatolia as a pretext, 'Abd al-Malik broke the treaty. The caliphate won a complete victory at the Battle of Sebastopolis in 692, in large part because the recently conscripted Slav troops deserted. The imperial position in Armenia subsequently collapsed, and Justinian II was deposed, mutilated, and exiled in 695. Leontius was proclaimed emperor, but in 698, the caliphate consummated its conquest of Ifriqiyah by taking Carthage, marking a definitive end to the Byzantine presence on the Mediterranean's southern shore.

The imperial fleet sent to relieve Carthage mutinied and proclaimed as emperor its commander, the *droungarios* Apsimar. When the garrison at Constantinople defected and opened the gates, Leontius was mutilated to disqualify him from the imperial throne and confined to a monastery, while Apsimar adopted the imperial name of Tiberius III.

In 701, Muhammad b. Marwān subdued Armenia in a campaign which, according to an indigenous account, left the population 'as if scorched by a smoking fire, and like a tuft of wheat trampled upon by swine'. In 703, the Armenians under Smbat Bagratuni rose up against Umayyad rule. 'Abd al-Malik dispatched his brother Muhammad, who negotiated a truce, then in 706, summoned the Armenian nobility to a conclave; once they were assembled, 'he confined them in a great church and set fire to it, thus incinerating them, and he allowed their women to be taken as spoil'.

Meanwhile, every summer, one or other of the sons of the caliph led an incursion into Byzantine territory. In 700, al-Walīd b. 'Abd al-Malik raided Asia Minor. In 701 and 703, it was the turn of 'Abd Allāh b. 'Abd al-Malik; he occupied Mopsuestia in Cilicia, which was transformed into a well-defended and menacing forward base. Tiberius's brother, Heraclius, defeated subsequent Arab encroachments, including a raid led by Yazīd b. Jubayr. But then the wheel turned again in Constantinople. In 705, Justinian II returned from exile and staged an unprecedented comeback

The ruins of the Medieval Armenian capital Ani now stand just across the border in Turkey from the modern nation of Armenia. In 705, the Armenians, struggling to hold out against the Umayyad caliphate, appealed to Constantinople for support. Emperor Justinian II dispatched an army, but the combined Byzantine/Armenian force was annihilated by Muhammad b. Marwān at Drashpet. The Arabs subsequently imposed tight control over Armenia. (Roland and Sabrina Michaud/akg-images)

The ruins of Anjar, an Umayyad stronghold, loom out of the morning mist in the Bekaa Valley, Lebanon. It was a fortified palace built in the early 8th century by the Umayyad caliph al-Walīd b. 'Abd al-Malik b. Marwān (r. 705–15) to serve the needs of a peripatetic court that was obligated to travel by the need to interact directly with key regional power brokers throughout the caliphate. (Author's collection)

as emperor. The key to his triumph was the support of Tervel, khan of the Bulgars. According to Theophanes, Justinian II made extravagant promises, 'even his own daughter as a wife. Tervel promised on oath to obey and cooperate with him in every way, and received him with honour.' The khan then 'raised his entire army, Bulgars and Slavs'. Once Justinian II was restored to the throne, he 'gave Tervel many presents (including imperial regalia) and sent him off in peace'.

The second reign of Justinian II would be a disaster for the Byzantine state. Not only was Tiberius executed, but so was his brother Heraclius, who was brought in chains before the throne, 'along with all the officers who were his comrades. Justinian hanged them all on the wall. He also sent men to the interior who routed out more officers and killed them, those who had been active against him and those who had not alike.' In his purges, Justinian II 'destroyed an uncountable number of political and military figures; many he gave bitter deaths by throwing them into the sea in sacks. He invited others to a fine meal and hanged some of them when they got up; others he cut down. Because of all this everyone was terrified.'

As the empire consumed itself, Arab raids on Anatolia intensified, and the imperial defences continued to give ground. In 708, Maslama b. 'Abd al-Malik, the brother of the caliph, finally eliminated the last stronghold of those Mardaites who remained unsubdued within the caliphate. In 709–10, Maslama and his nephew, al-'Abbas b. al-Walīd, laid siege to Tyana. The emperor dispatched a relief force under Theodore Karteroukas and Theophylaktos Salibas. 'But the two generals squabbled with each other, engaged the Arabs in a disorderly way, and were routed', Theophanes records. 'Many thousands were destroyed, and many taken prisoner. The Arabs, once they had taken the army's baggage-train and food-supply, could lay siege to Tyana until they captured it. They had been short of food and intended to withdraw.' On terms, the inhabitants abandoned the town, 'which has been a wasteland until the present. The Arabs did not abide by the treaty, but exiled them to the desert; they also enslaved many of them.' Maslama and al-'Abbas subsequently divided their forces and campaigned in Byzantine territory. Al-'Abbas raided Cilicia and from there turned west as far as Dorylaion, while Maslama seized the fortresses of Kamouliana and Heraclea Cybistra before marching west to take Nicomedia, some of his troops raiding Chrysopolis opposite Constantinople itself.

Justinian II meanwhile transferred the thematic cavalry to Thrace, outfitted a naval expedition, and broke the peace with the Bulgars, only to be routed in the subsequent battle. Finally, when the emperor dispatched a punitive expedition to Cherson in 711, the fleet mutinied, proclaimed an exiled officer (Bardanes) emperor, and sailed to Constantinople. Justinian II left to raise troops in the Opsikion and Armeniakon Themes, but they abandoned him to his fate. Bardanes, who had adopted the imperial name Philippicus, executed Justinian II and his son, bringing a final, bloody end to the dynasty of Heraclius.

Taking advantage of this chaos, the Arabs were seizing and garrisoning strongholds as they advanced. Camacha, commanding the eastern terminus of a major highway, was occupied in 711. The empire was now coming under immense pressure on both of its flanks. In 712–13, the Bulgars 'reached the Golden Gate after capturing all of Thrace, and then returned unharmed to their own country with uncountable flocks', Theophanes relates. Meanwhile, as recorded in the doleful annual accounts of Agapius, the Arab pressure was relentless. Maslama took 'Amaseia and many other fortresses' in one raid; al-'Abbās b. al-Walīd captured Antioch in Pisidia in another; Uthmān b. Hayyān al-Murri raided into Cilicia, 'forced many fortresses there to capitulate and took the inhabitants into captivity in Syria'. Then it was Maslama again, as he 'penetrated into Galatia, captured many fortresses and took the population into captivity'.

Philippicus undertook preparations to counter these raids, but in 713 the soldiers of the Opsikion Theme mutinied. The emperor was deposed and blinded, and the *protoasekretis* Artemius, a palatine clerical official, became emperor as Anastasius II. He dispatched an embassy to Damascus, ostensibly to discuss peace terms, but in reality to ascertain the caliph's intentions. His diplomats reported the caliphate was massing both land and naval forces for a combined operation against Constantinople.

Anastasius II immediately began preparations. He commanded that every resident in Constantinople be able to pay his own way for three years' time, and ordered those unable to do so to abandon the city. He expanded the navy, restored the land and sea walls, outfitting them with artillery, and built up the reserves in the imperial granaries. In addition to these precautions, Anastasius II was also determined to be proactive. A naval force was fitted out in an attempt to pre-empt the blockade

A gold solidus of Emperor Philippicus (r.711–13), who assumed the throne in chaotic circumstances. With Khazar support, the Byzantine outpost in the Crimea, Cherson, rebelled in 710 and 711 and proclaimed an exiled Armenian, Bardanes, as emperor with the regnal name Philippicus. Justinian II led the army in person to the east, but the rebel forces persuaded the emperor's men to desert him and Justinian was executed. Philippicus' reign was a complete failure, and he was deposed and replaced by Anastasius II. (Classic Numismatic Group LLC, https://www.cngcoins.com/)

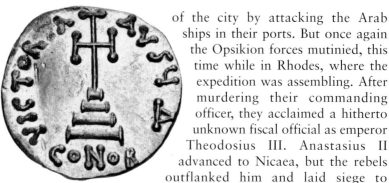

Emperor Anastasius II (r. 713–15), depicted on a gold solidus. Originally a court functionary by the name of Artemius, he was elevated to the throne when the army of the Opsikion Theme overthrew Emperor Philippicus. These same troops later turned against him, and he was forced to abdicate. (Classic Numismatic Group LLC, https://www.cngcoins.com/)

of the city by attacking the Arab ships in their ports. But once again the Opsikion forces mutinied, this time while in Rhodes, where the expedition was assembling. After murdering their commanding officer, they acclaimed a hitherto unknown fiscal official as emperor Theodosius III. Anastasius II advanced to Nicaea, but the rebels outflanked him and laid siege to Constantinople, where the insurgent and loyalist fleets 'fought with each other daily for six months'. Finally, agents for Theodosius III succeeded in opening the gate of the Blacharnae to the rebels, who stormed the city that night, 'sparing no-one and working great destruction'. Anastasius II, who had sent an appeal to the caliph via the commander of the invading armies, Maslama, for military help against the usurper, abdicated and retired as a monk to Thessaloniki.

His successor, Theodosius III, occupied the throne for just over 12 months. His major contribution to the empire's security was to agree a treaty favourable to the Bulgar khan Tervel in an effort to secure his support against – or at least, neutrality towards – the imminent Arab invasion. Under its terms, the extant borders were recognized, Constantinople conceding these stretched from the Gulf of Burgas on the Black Sea coast through northern Thrace to Maritsa on the Aegean; the annual tribute agreed to in 679 by Constantine IV and confirmed by Justinian II was reaffirmed; and Bulgar merchants gained official access to Europe's largest market in Constantinople.

While welcome, this initiative was not much to set against decades of defeat and chronic instability. As it approached its ultimate trial, the empire seemed more fixated on recrimination than renewal. Contemporary accounts like the *Chronicle of John of Nikiu* and the *Armenian History* describe a world where central imperial power was gradually receding, creating a power vacuum. 'For you all know what clouds of dust the Devil stirred up,' wrote the author of the *Miracles of Saint Demetriu*s, 'when he smothered love and sowed mutual hatred in all the East, in Cilicia, in Asia, in Palestine and the neighbouring lands up to Constantinople itself.'

Of all the emperors who assumed the Byzantine throne, none can have been as obscure, or more reluctant, than Theodosius III (r. 715–17). A provincial bureaucrat pressed into the role by the troops of the Opsikion Theme, who were in revolt against Anastasius II, the only significant achievement of his reign was a truce and treaty with the Bulgars. He abdicated in favour of Leo III. (Classic Numismatic Group LLC, https://www.cngcoins.com/)

CHRONOLOGY

602   Murder of Byzantine emperor Maurice and usurpation of Phocas. Over the next two decades the Sasanian Persians under Khosrow II take Syria, Egypt, and Armenia; the Avars and Slavs overrun the Balkans.

610   Execution of Phocas; Heraclius emperor. Muhammad begins to proselytize Islam in Mecca.

622   Heraclius defeats the Sasanians in Anatolia. Hijrah: Muslim emigration to Medina.

624   Battle of Badr; Muslims defeat Meccans.

625   Battle of Uhud; Meccans defeat Muslims.

626   Sasanian and Avar–Slav siege of Constantinople defeated.

627   Battle of Nineveh; Heraclius defeats the Sasanians. Battle of the Trench; Muslims defeat Meccans.

628   Deposition and murder of Khosrow II; end of the Byzantine-Sasanian war.

629   Muslims take Mecca.

632   Death of Muhammad; Abū Bakr *amir al-mu'minin*.

634   Death of Abū Bakr; 'Umar b. al-Khattāb *amir al-mu'minin*.

636   Battle of Yarmouk; Arabs defeat Byzantines. Battle of al-Qādisiyyah; Arabs defeat Sasanians.

637   Arabs take Jerusalem, Antioch, and Aleppo from the Byzantines, and Ctesiphon from the Sasanians.

641   Death of Heraclius; Constans II emperor.

642   Arabs take Alexandria. Battle of Nāhavand; Arabs defeat Sasanians.

644   Murder of 'Umar; 'Uthmān b. al-Khattab *amir al-mu'minin*.

651   Arabs take Merv; death of Yazdegerd III; end of Sasanian dynasty.

654   Battle of the Masts; Arab fleet destroys Byzantine navy. Crete and Rhodes pillaged. Mu'āwiya invades Anatolia. First Arab siege of Constantinople defeated.

656   Murder of 'Uthmān b. al-Khattab; Alī b. Abi-Talib *amir al-mu'minin*. First *fitna*. Battle of the Camel; Alī defeats 'Ā'ishah.

657   Battle of Siffin; Mu'āwiya faces down Alī.

661   Assassination of Alī; Mu'āwiya caliph; end of the First *fitna*.

667   Arabs occupy Chalcedon.

668–69 Murder of Constans II; Constantine IV emperor. Second Arab siege of Constantinople defeated.

670   Arabs occupy Cyzicus.

674   Third Arab siege of Constantinople defeated.

677   Byzantine naval counterattack links up with Mardaite resistance in Lebanon.

680   Bulgars defeat Byzantines at Messembria. Death of Mu'āwiya; Yazīd caliph. Arabs sign 30-year truce with Byzantines. Battle of Karbala; death of Husayn b. Alī.

683   Second *fitna*. Death of Yazīd; Mu'āwiya II caliph.

684   Death of Mu'āwiya II; Marwān caliph.

685	Death of Constantine IV; Justinian II emperor. Death of Marwān; 'Abd al-Malik caliph. Arabs recommit to truce with Byzantines.
692	Fall of Mecca; death of 'Abd Allāh b. al-Zubayr; end of the second *fitna*. Battle of Sebastopolis; Arabs defeat Byzantines.
695	Justinian II deposed; Leontius emperor.
698	Arabs take Carthage. Leontius deposed; Tiberius III emperor.
705	Tiberius III deposed; Justinian II emperor. Death of 'Abd al-Malik; al-Walīd b. 'Abd al-Malik caliph.
711	Justinian II deposed; Philippicus emperor. Battle of Guadalete; Arabs defeat Visigoths.
712	Arabs take Samarqand.
713	Philippicus deposed; Anastasius II emperor.
715	Anastasius II deposed; Theodosius III emperor. Death of al-Walīd b. 'Abd al-Malik; Sulaymān b. al-Malik caliph.
716	Maslama crosses the Taurus frontier, sacks Sardis and Pergamum, and winters on imperial territory.
25 March 717	Leo III crowned emperor.
15 August 717	Maslama with the caliphal army arrives at Constantinople.
1 September 717	Sulaymān b. Mu'ad with the caliphal fleet arrives at Constantinople.
24 September 717	Death of Sulaymān; 'Umar b. al-'Azīz caliph.
8 October 717	Death of Sulaymān b. Mu'ad.
15 August 718	Maslama withdraws his forces; fourth Arab siege of Constantinople defeated.

732	Battle of Poitiers; Franks defeat Arabs.
741	Death of Leo III; Constantine V emperor.
750	Battle of the Zab; Abbasids overthrow the Umayyads.
827	Saracens conquer Crete.
831	Saracens take Palermo.
838	Abbasids sack Amorium.
840	Saracens take Taranto.
843	Saracens take Messina.
846	Saracens raid Rome.
849	Saracens take Bari.
853	Byzantine naval expedition sacks Damietta.
860	First Rus' expedition against Constantinople.
863	Two decisive Byzantine victories over Saracen incursions in Anatolia.
869	Saracens take Malta.
871	Latins retake Bari.
873	Byzantines retake Samosata.
878	Saracens take Syracuse.
896	Bulgars defeat Byzantines at Bulgarophygon.
902	Saracens conquer Sicily.
1071	Seljuk Turks defeat Byzantines at Manzikert.
1086	Almoravids defeat a Christian coalition at Sagrajas.
1095	Pope Urban II preaches the First Crusade.

OPPOSING COMMANDERS

LEO III

The 11th-century *Kitāb al-'Uyun* (*Book of Springs*) relates the 'wonderful story … of the fortunes of Leo, and his renown and his valour', and how he rose to become emperor. Leo's sobriquet, and that for the dynasty he founded, is Isaurian, but in fact, he was born *c*.680, 'a Christian inhabitant of Mar'ash [Germanicia, contemporary Kahramanmaraş], where to this day there is a celebrated church called after him'. Another Arab account, the *Zuqnin Chronicle*, also describes Leo as 'a courageous, strong, and warlike man … by origin a Syrian'.

Germanicia was taken by the Rashidun Arabs in 645 and, in common with many of the Christian communities transferred to imperial territory during the population exchanges sponsored by Justinian II, his family was forcefully resettled, in his case to Mesembria on the Black Sea coast of Thrace.

Originally named Konon, he enters history in 705, the year Justinian II marched on Constantinople to reclaim his throne. Leo boldly rode out to meet him, offering 500 sheep as provisions for the exiled emperor's entourage. In return, he was invited to join the imperial guard with the rank of *spatharius*. In 710, when he was about 35 years old, Leo was sent on a military and diplomatic mission to the Caucasus Mountains. His task was to incite an attack by the Alans, a Byzantine ally, on the neighbouring Abasgians, who had transferred their allegiance to the caliphate. Overcoming obstacles ranging from cloak-and-dagger intrigue to a trek across wintry mountains in snowshoes, Leo succeeded in his assignment. In 715, Leo was appointed *stratêgos* of the Anatolikan Theme by Anastasius II. When that emperor was deposed later the same year, Leo owed no loyalty to the usurper, Theodosius III. Maslama's invasion of Anatolia the following year offered Leo the chance to make his own bid for the throne. It was a perilous choice: the path to power was unclear, failure would mean death, and there was no guarantee the dysfunctional empire could be redeemed from its downward

This gold solidus features Leo III (r. 717–41) on the obverse and his son and eventual successor as Constantine V on the reverse. Leo was a lawmaker as well as a warrior. Leo recodified Byzantine law in his *Ecloga*, the first revision to the legal framework since Justinian's code of 529. Significantly, in recognition of the empire's shifting identity, the new laws were written in Greek instead of the hitherto official language Latin. (Classic Numismatic Group LLC, https://www.cngcoins.com/)

spiral into oblivion even if he succeeded. But he had significant assets that made the attempt plausible. Leo was in the prime of life; he was widely travelled; we can assume he was at least bilingual, in Arab and Greek; he had honed his negotiating skills on diplomatic assignments for the empire; and he was an experienced military administrator. By all evidence, he was acutely intelligent, a shrewd judge of character, charming when he wanted to be, and authoritative when required to be so. He was the right man in the right place, and his convoluted path to power would prove one of the hinges of fate in world history.

So why does he remain so obscure? The answer lies in the events of 726. At the heart of Constantinople, looming over the Bronze Gate (*Chalkē*), the main entrance to the palace, was a massive golden icon of Jesus, the so-called Christ Chalkites. It was in that year the citizens of the capital were shocked and then horrified to witness a detachment of palace guards deliberately and systematically smash this religious and artistic treasure to the ground. A group of women actually lynched the officer responsible for such desecration, and only the arrival of reinforcements suppressed the eruption of a full-fledged riot.

This was no mere incident of random vandalism but an act of state policy at the express command of the emperor himself. In pondering the catastrophes that had befallen his empire over the past century, Leo had concluded they were the direct outcome of the state and its people having lost the favour of God. The primary factor in this withdrawal of the divine aegis was the increasingly flagrant violation of the Second Commandment – 'No graven images or likenesses' – at all levels of society. Icons throughout the empire had become objects of fetishistic veneration in their own right. This blatant idolatry was particularly distressing in comparison to the stark doctrinal clarity of Islam. By beginning with the icon most associated with the emperor himself, Leo had sent a clear message; starting from the top down, he intended to purify Byzantine culture of this contamination, root and branch.

But attachment to icons was too deep-rooted in the Byzantine psyche for such a policy to work. Beyond destroying untold priceless works of art, creating a host of martyrs, provoking a rift with the Curia in Rome, and destabilizing the social fabric generally, Leo's iconoclasm, implemented on and off by his successors until it was finally abandoned in 843, ultimately accomplished nothing beyond costing him the prominence he had earned in the pages of history.

What records we have from this period are almost exclusively derived from sources with an ecclesiastical background. The fact mainstream religious authorities were unalterably opposed to state intervention in their affairs ensured that Leo would be 'known to posterity by the invectives of his enemies', Edward Gibbon comments. Foremost amongst these was the primary chronicler of the era, Theophanes. To him, 'God's foe Leo' was 'totally ignorant and stupid', 'a bloody man ... tyrant ... wild beast' and 'lawbreaking emperor' who, 'Like his teachers the Arabs', 'raged against the true faith' through promulgation of the 'malignant, illegal, and evil ... abominable, wicked doctrine' of iconoclasm. 'Saracen-minded Leo,' Theophanes concluded, 'was under the control of his Arab heart.' This last barb suggests that, throughout his reign, there remained an undercurrent of chauvinism within the upper echelons of Byzantine society against Leo for his provincial, Arab, origins.

This was scant reward for the man who, armed with nothing more than his innate talent and ambition, had risen in the space of 12 years from Syrian peasant refugee to supreme power and led the empire through its greatest trial.

MASLAMA B. 'ABD. AL-MALIK

No empire, no dynasty, can have benefitted from the services of a more loyal general than Maslama b. 'Abd al-Malik. Maslama was the son of the Umayyad caliph 'Abd al-Malik b. al-Marwān (r. 685–705), which made him half-brother of the caliphs al-Walid I (r. 705–15), Sulaymān (r. 715–17), Yazīd II (r. 720–24), and Hishām b. 'Abd al-Malik (r. 724–43). Maslama himself was excluded from the line of succession as his mother was a low-born concubine. Yet he served the caliphate in field commands at the highest level with honour and distinction for more than a quarter of a century without a whisper of dissent or disloyalty. Maslama was renowned as the consummate military professional, lean and tanned from years of near constant campaigning ('that yellow locust', as Yazīd b. al-Muhallab called him). He is first mentioned as leading, along with his nephew, al-'Abbas b. al-Walīd, the annual summer campaign (ṣawa'if) against the Byzantines in 705.

Maslama's defining quality was his ironclad code of honour. In 706, an invasion of Cilicia led by Maimun al-Gurgunami ('Maimun the Mardaite') was defeated by a Byzantine army under a general named Marianus near Tyana. According to Baladhuri, Maimun had been a slave of the caliph Mū'awiya's sister, who had fled to the Mardaites. After the Mardaites had been subdued, Maslama, hearing of his valour, liberated him and entrusted him with a military command, and later swore to avenge his death. As a result, Maslama, again in partnership with al-'Abbas, took Tyana after a nine-month siege over the winter of 709/10, defeating a Byzantine relief force in the process, and razing the city to the ground in the aftermath.

Having already taken office as emir of Jund Qinnasrin in northern Syria, Maslama was appointed emir of Armenia and Azerbaijan, succeeding his uncle Muhammad b. Marwān, effectively giving him complete control of the caliphate's entire north-western frontier. From this position he launched several campaigns against the Byzantines, devastating Galatia and sacking

This coin depicts the fifth Umayyad caliph 'Abd al-Mālik b. Marwān b. al-Hakam, seated alongside the founder of the dynasty Mū'awiya b. Abū Sufyan. When the caliphate was plunged into a second *fitna* in 680, it was 'Abd al-Mālik who reasserted central authority, reestablishing the Umayyad dynasty's monopoly on power that would endure until 750. (Classic Numismatic Group LLC, https://www.cngcoins.com/)

These ruins are all that remains of Pliska, the capital founded by the Bulgar khan Asparukh after he pushed south of the Danube in 680. The Bulgars were the wild card in the conflict between the Byzantine Empire and Umayyad caliphate. Their intervention would be critical to the outcome of the siege of Constantinople in 717–18. (akg-images/De Agostini Picture Lib./A. Vergani)

Amaseia in 712, and taking Melitene in 714. He also pushed north of the Caucasus, provoking a conflict with the Khazars. In 710, and again in 714, he marched on the pass at Derbent (Bab al-Abwab, the 'Gate of Gates'), which he took and destroyed during the latter expedition. With his experience and credentials in administration, strategic planning, and tactical operations, he was the logical choice to command the grand expedition against Constantinople.

After the death of caliph 'Umar and the accession of his brother, Yazīd II, in 720, Maslama was tasked with the suppression of the revolt of Yazīd b. al-Muhallab, whom he defeated and killed in August 720. He nevertheless was forced into retirement by the caliph because Maslama favoured his brother Hishām for the succession over Yazīd II's son Walīd.

Maslama was rehabilitated after Yazīd's death. In winter 725, he led an expedition against Asia Minor from Melitene, which culminated in the sack of Caesarea on 13 January 726. From 727, he fought a grinding war of attrition against the Khazars before being replaced in 729 by al-Jarrāh b. 'Abd Allāh al-Hakamī. Theophanes holds him responsible for a raid into Cappadocia, 'where he took the fortress of Kharsianon by treachery' in late 730, but Arab sources credit Mū'awiya b. Hishām (son of Hishām b. 'Abd al-Malik) for this achievement.

After the defeat and death of al-Jarrāh on 9 December 730, Maslama was again appointed emir of Armenia and Azerbaijan in order to stabilize the situation in the Caucasus. He succeeded in defeating the Khazar khagan, killing his son in the process, and recovered Derbent, which he reorganized as a military colony (*misr*), resettling it with 24,000 soldiers. However, dissatisfaction with his progress led to his being replaced on 3 March 732 by his cousin and protégé Marwān b. Muhammad. Maslama subsequently retired from public life, presumably to his extensive estates in northern Syria. He died on 24 December 738.

Had Maslama succeeded in his supreme challenge of taking Constantinople, his name would be proverbial in the annals of warfare. But this one accomplishment, in a career that spanned decades of consistent achievement beforehand and afterwards, was beyond him. Although for this reason he does not quite rank in the top tier of military commanders, the Byzantines never confronted a more dedicated, professional, or determined foe in the field. His defeat can be ascribed to a number of variables. Some of these were beyond his control, from the inherent impregnability of Constantinople to the defection of the Coptic crews in the resupply fleets. But some contingencies should have been anticipated. The Arabs had already experienced the destructive power of Greek Fire; countermeasures in tactics or technology should have been arrived at beforehand. The potential influence of the Bulgars, one way or the other, appears to have been completely overlooked in planning for the campaign. Had they been brought over to his side, Maslama could have found their support adding irresistible impetus to his assault. Had they at least been bribed into neutrality, Maslama would have enjoyed greater security and freedom of action. But the caliphs had always disdained forging alliances with unbelievers; why enter into any accommodation with a people destined to be absorbed into the *Dar-al-Islam* anyway after the inevitable fall of Constantinople? This hubris was to prove extremely costly. Finally, Maslama's fatal flaw was his persistence in believing, despite clear and ever-mounting evidence, that Leo remained secretly his client and was only waiting for the right moment to surrender the city. The longer Leo delayed, the more desperate Maslama seems to have become to cling to this illusion, well past the point of rationality. Perhaps once he appreciated the strength of the defences arrayed against him, he lost hope of ever overcoming them other than through treachery from within. Perhaps his own sense of honour would not allow him to assume Leo was anything other than operating in good faith. Perhaps having convinced himself of his genius in foisting a puppet emperor on the Byzantines, he could not accept having been in fact outwitted.

Whatever his motivation, the narrative of the *Kitāb al-'Uyun* best sums up both the strength and fatal flaw of his character when it concludes: 'Maslama was powerless, with no counsel in him for the war, nor among his companions was there any man at his disposal with any counsel in him; yet he was a valiant man.'

A gold dinar of the fifth Umayyad caliph 'Abd al-Mālik b. Marwān al-Hakam (r. 685–705). During his reign, Arabic became the only official language of administration, replacing Greek and Persian. As a component of his policy of islamization, 'Abd al-Mālik ordered construction of the Dome of the Rock in Jerusalem. He also reformed the currency, all images being replaced by text quoting the Ikhlās Qur'an sura that 'God has not begotten and is not begotten', an open challenge to the Christian concept of the incarnation. Deliberately or otherwise, this provoked the collapse of the extant truce between the caliphate and the empire that had held since 680. (Classic Numismatic Group LLC, https://www.cngcoins.com/)

OPPOSING FORCES AND PLANS

ARAB

The western canon of the great commanders in military history includes such names as Alexander, Hannibal, and Caesar. It has no place for the campaigns of Khālid b. al-Walīd in Syria; 'Amr b. al-'As in Egypt; Sa'd b. Abī Waqqās in Iraq; Uqba b. Nāfi in North Africa; Ṭāriq b. Ziyād and Musa b. Nusayr in Spain; Qutaybah b. Muslim in Transoxiana; or Muḥammad b. Qāsim ath-Thaqafī in Sind. But these were the men who, between the death of the Prophet Muhammad in 632 and the Battle of Poitiers in 732, forged an empire that stretched from the Punjab to the Pyrenees, from Kabul to Casablanca. There was no precedent in history for conquest on this scale in terms of its timeframe, dimensions, or transformative cultural impact, and there would be only one subsequent parallel – not the transient Mongol khanate of the 13th century, but the empire-building of the Spanish in the New World.

These achievements have been overlooked because there is no place for them in the established worldviews of Western historians. To the right, the

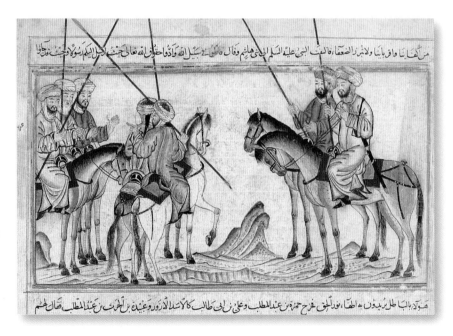

The marshalling of the faithful prior to the Battle of Badr (624). This miniature painting from Rashīd al-Dīn Ṭabīb's *Jāmi' al-tawārīkh* dates from the early 14th century and contains anachronisms (such as the horses being outfitted with stirrups) but does emphasize the significance of cavalry in early Islamic warfare, and the mobility of the lightly armed and armoured warriors who would subsequently conquer half the known world. Note also the figure on the right carries a sword with a straight blade; the curved scimitar so closely associated with the Middle East evolved in a later era. (akg-images/Pictures From History)

Anatolia, 715–18

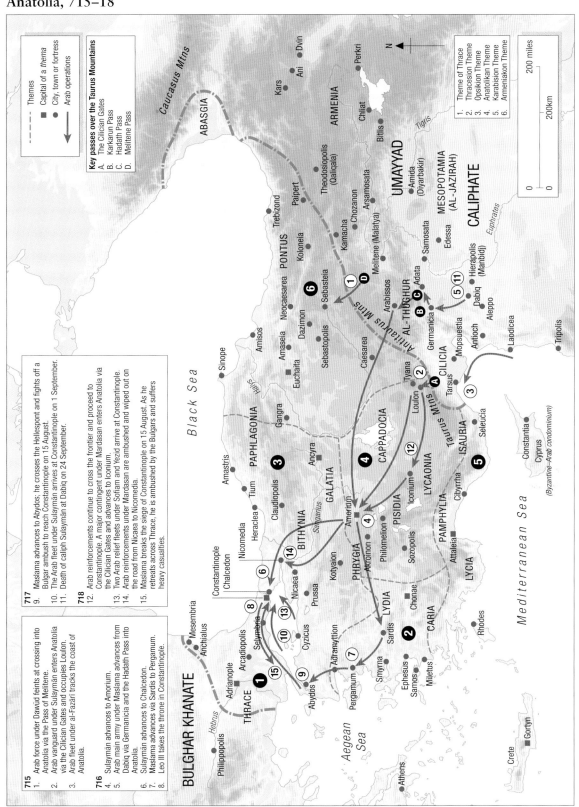

Themes
- - - - - Themes
■ Capital of a *thema*
● City, town or fortress
→ Arab operations

Key passes over the Taurus Mountains
A. The Cilician Gates
B. Karkarun Pass
C. Hadath Pass
D. Melitene Pass

1. Theme of Thrace
2. Thracesion Theme
3. Opsikion Theme
4. Anatolikan Theme
5. Karabision Theme
6. Armeniakon Theme

200 miles
200km

N

715
1. Arab force under Dawūd feints at crossing into Anatolia via the Pass of Melitene.
2. Arab vanguard under Sulaymān enters Anatolia via the Cilician Gates and occupies Loulon.
3. Arab fleet under al-Fazārī tracks the coast of Anatolia.

716
4. Sulaymān advances to Amorium.
5. Arab main army under Maslama advances from Dabiq via Germanicia and the Hadath Pass into Anatolia.
6. Sulaymān advances to Chalcedon.
7. Maslama advances via Sardis to Pergamum.
8. Leo III takes the throne in Constantinople.

717
9. Maslama advances to Abydos; he crosses the Hellespont and fights off a Bulgar ambush to reach Constantinople on 15 August.
10. Arab vanguard under Sulaymān enters Anatolia via the Cilician Gates and occupies Loulon.
11. The Arab fleet under Sulaymān arrives at Constantinople on 1 September. Death of caliph Sulaymān at Dabiq on 24 September.

718
12. Arab reinforcements continue to cross the frontier and proceed to Constantinople. A major contingent under Mardasan enters Anatolia via the Cilician Gates and advances to Iconium.
13. Two Arab relief fleets under Sofiam and Yezid arrive at Constantinople.
14. Arab reinforcements under Mardasan are ambushed and wiped out on the road from Nicaea to Nicomedia.
15. Maslama breaks the siege of Constantinople on 15 August. As he retreats across Thrace, he is ambushed by the Bulgars and suffers heavy casualties.

Early Islamic architecture is expressed in the Qasr-al-Kharana, which dates to the Umayyad era. The structure comprises two storeys of residential units arranged around a central courtyard. The exact purpose of this building – whether military, commercial, or diplomatic – remains unclear. Although commonly referred to as a castle, it appears to be more of a symbolic representation of one, and the best guess is it served as an occasional meeting place for the local Bedouin tribes to convene with representatives of the governing Umayyad dynasty. (Graham Hobster/Pixabay)

rise and reign of the caliphs is an embarrassing contradiction to its thesis of white supremacy and the innate superiority of the assumed 'Western way of war'. Conversely, to the left, Muslims can only be the victims, not the instigators, of imperialist aggression. Islam's interaction with the West, therefore, begins with its being subjected to the unprovoked proto-capitalist colonization of the Crusades. The preceding four-and-a-half centuries are passed over in silence.

'The Qur'an does not sanctify warfare,' Karen Armstrong insists: 'There was nothing religious about these campaigns.' But Islam was born fighting for its existence. Muhammad had personally led the believers into battle at Badr (624) and Uhud (625), and fighting for the faith is expressly sanctified in the Qur'an: 'Let those who would trade this life for the hereafter fight in God's path; and We will recompense well whomsoever does fight in God's path, whether he dies or achieves victory.'

This ethos was ingrained in Arab imperialism, manifested from the beginning, at the Battle of Mu'tah in 629, the first clash between Islam and the West, when Muhammad dispatched an expedition north to probe Byzantine defences in the Transjordan. 'Abd Allāh b. Rawāḥah, one of the earliest converts and most fervid believers, was undismayed by the spectacle of the much larger force arrayed against them. 'Do we rely on our numbers or the virtue of our faith?' he cried indignantly. 'Victory, or martyrdom and paradise – we must surely win the one or the other.'

When battle commenced, Zayd b. Ḥārithah, the Prophet's adopted son, bearing the white banner which Muhammad himself had entrusted to him, plunged into the midst of the enemy's ranks until transfixed by their spears. Ja'far b. Abī Ṭālib, older brother of Alī, Muhammad's son-in-law, seized the banner and, crying 'How wonderful is paradise as it draws near!' raised it once more. Tradition relates that, when both his hands were cut off, he continued to hold the banner aloft between his two stumps until he was hacked down. Many martyrs fell that day, including 'Abd Allāh b. Rawāḥah, before Khālid b. al-Walīd rallied the survivors in a fighting withdrawal.

That the believers were dedicated to remaking the world in the cause of Islam was a core article of Arab faith and identity. According to Sayyid

Qutb, if any of the faithful had been asked for what they were fighting, 'none would have answered, "My country is in danger; I am fighting for its defence," or "The Persians and the Romans have come upon us," or "We want to extend our dominion and want more spoils."' Their mission was to propagate the faith, 'to bring anyone who wishes from servitude to men into the service of God alone … and from the tyranny of religions into the justice of Islam'. Submission was the only correct path, 'and we fight with those who rebel until we are martyred or become victorious'.

Subsequent generations of Arab conquerors would live – and die – by these precepts, and by the Hadith, recorded by al-Bukhari, that 'paradise lies under the shades of swords'. Consider Uqba b. Nāfi, vanquisher of the Maghreb in north-west Africa, who crossed the Atlas Mountains in 670 and was the first Muslim to lay eyes on the Atlantic Ocean. As the 14th-century Andalusian historian b. Idhāri al-Marrākushi relates, Uqba rode his horse into the surf, crying out: 'Oh God, if the sea had not prevented me, I would have galloped on forever like Alexander the Great, upholding your faith and fighting the unbelievers!' That the religious imperative persisted into the Umayyad era is confirmed by the publication in the 8th century of scholarly justifications for jihad, including the *Kitāb al-Siyar* of Abū Ishāq al-Fazārī and the *Kitāb al-Jihād* of 'Abd Allāh b. al-Mubārak (who practised what he preached; a devout participant in *razzias* against the imperial enemy, Arab accounts describe how he would 'bellow like a bull or cow being slaughtered' in combat). Another preacher of jihad on the Anatolian frontier, Alī b. Bakr, was once 'wounded in battle, so that his entrails came spilling out onto his saddle. He stuffed them back in, using his turban as a bandage to bind them in place, and then proceeded to kill 13 of the enemy', to cries of 'Allahu Akbar!' A fighter in the jihad was termed a *mujahid*; any who fell in the fulfillment of his duty in the path of Allah earned the status of martyr (*shahid*).

Tempered by a harsh climate, the Arabs had always been skilled fighters, who revelled in their prestige in war. A poem ascribed to 'Amir b. al-Tufayl, a contemporary of the Prophet Muhammad, expresses this attitude beautifully:

> We came upon their host in the morning, and they were like a flock
> of sheep upon whom falls the ravening wolf …
> We fell on them with white steel ground to keenness; we cut them to
> pieces until they were destroyed
> And we carried off their women on the saddles behind us, with their
> cheeks bleeding, torn in anguish by their nails.
> Truly war knows that I am her child.

Historically, the only weakness of the Arabs had been their division. Their new faith had forged them into a war machine with limitless potential, as b. Khaldun confirms: 'The combination of a tribal solidarity and a religious drive is overwhelming.'

An Umayyad spearhead, dating from the 8th century. Arab armies sported two types of spear. The longer *rumh* was essentially an infantry weapon with a wooden haft and a metal head, allowing it to be used as a slashing as well as a stabbing weapon. The shorter *harbah* may have been used on horseback, but in a secondary role; as 9th-century Islamic scholar al Jahiz put it, 'the strength of the horseman rests in the strength of his hand and the length and breadth of his sword'. (Time Vault Gallery)

The first phase of the conquests was impelled by tribal leaders (*ru'us al-qaba'il*) and their personal retinues, settled in encampments or towns (*amsār*), enrolled in a central register (*dīwān*), and rewarded according to a system based, at least in principle, on gift rather than compensation.

As the caliphate expanded, the basic Arabian tribal unit (*ashira*) proved too small to provide an effective operational formation, making reorganization and professionalism imperative. This was accomplished by the Umayyad caliphs through the establishment of regional armies known as *junds*, organized around fortified provincial cities, the first being Damascus in Syria, Tiberias in Jordan, and Jerusalem, Ascalon, and Homs in Palestine. As Islam swept across south-west Asia and North Africa, new *junds* appeared with non-Arab Muslim converts (*mawali*) forming the majority of the Muslim armies, although Arab Muslims, especially those from Arabia and Syria, made up the officer corps, with senior members of the Umayyad family often holding command positions and subsequently serving as emirs.

After the transition from amateur warrior to professional soldier (*muqatila*), armies were maintained by the state, a fixed proportion of taxes and rents being allocated for the military budget via the *dīwān al-jund*. Soldiers on active duty had their regular monthly salary (*atā*) supplemented by the booty won during a campaign on their own behalf (*ghahnima*), and by the official share of the spoils (*fay*) distributed by the government. Regular forces were supplemented by slave (*ghulam*) and volunteer (*ghazi*) units.

In the wake of the Byzantine collapse at Yarmouk, Jerusalem (with its myriad sites of veneration, such as the Tomb of the Virgin pictured here) was isolated and indefensible. After a siege of six months, the city surrendered intact and on terms in April 637 to the *amir al-mu'minin* 'Umar himself. The surrounding country was not pacified so benignly, with many thousands slaughtered. (Author's collection)

Actions included battle (*mujarrada*), reconnaissance (*tali'a*), localized raiding (*sari'a*), independent long-range raiding (*jarida*) and mobile garrison duty (*rabita*). In battle, infantry were drawn up in ranks (*sufuf*) in close formation (*tabi'a*). The *khamis* (five-division) model for line of battle included the *muqaddama* (advance guard), *qalb* (centre), *maimanah* (right wing), *maisarah* (left wing) and *saqah* (rearguard). Muslim light (*mujarrada*) and heavy (*mujaffafa*) cavalry operated on the wings or through the centre, making flanking or encircling movements to exploit opportunities created once the infantry had disrupted the enemy's line.

Rapid attack and withdrawal (*karr wa farr*) remained the most common manoeuvre and, reflecting Arab tradition, infantry archers remained the most important arm. In battle the archers would kneel in the front rank, with shield and spear-armed infantry behind them and cavalry to the rear and flanks.

Umayyad armies were well organized, disciplined, and equipped. Even the hostile account of Theodosius Grammaticus, gloating over ultimate Byzantine victory, in no way downplays the magnitude of the threat presented by such a redoubtable foe:

> Where now, oh cursed ones, are your shining-bright ranks of arrows; where
> now the melodious chords of bow-strings? Where is the glitter of your swords
> and spears, your breastplates and head-borne helmets, scimitars and darkened
> shields? Where are the ... arrows and spears, the banners, fiery-red or black?

The principal weapons were sword (*saif*), worn from a baldric, and javelin
(*harbah*). Shields were either large (*turs*), a wood and leather composite, or
small (*daraqa*), comprised entirely of leather. Protection for the head included
the *mighfar*, known to the West as an aventail, a hood of chainmail, and a
rounded helmet called the *bayda*, swathed in a turban. Both infantry and
cavalry wore chainmail or lamellar armour beneath clothing woven from camel
wool and patterned in bright shades of scarlet, red, blue, yellow, green, and
especially white, the Umayyad colour. Insignia included *tiraz*, armbands woven
in coloured silk bearing embroidered inscriptions, often from the Qur'an.

Arab commanders generally shied away from undertaking the siege of
a fortified city, preferring to retain the initiative in open country so as to
maximize the strategic options available through their mobility. Subterfuge
or other gambits could be seized upon if the opportunity arose. For example,
after investing the Armenian city of Dvin for five days in 642, the Arabs
launched an assault, 'and it fell to them; for they had shrouded it in clouds
of smoke and, by this means and by arrow shots, they drove back the men
who were defending the ramparts. Then, having set up their ladders, they
climbed on to the walls, hurled themselves into the square, and opened the
gates.' Nevertheless, Arabic siegecraft was quite sophisticated, incorporating
both the small pole-framed trebuchet (*'arrādāh*), 20 of which were deployed
during the 637 siege of Ctesiphon by Sa'd b. Abī Waqqās, and its larger
trestle-framed equivalent (*manjanīq*), one of which, requiring a 500-man
crew and dubbed 'The Bride', was used during the 710 siege of Daybul
in Sind.

Umayyad logistics in support of such far-flung campaigns was critical
to operational success, and the supply chains established were testament to
the resources and proficiency available to the caliphate. 'I have seen us on
summer expeditions [against the Byzantines],' wrote Qays b. al-Haytham
to his fellow veterans of such endeavours, 'each one of us in charge of a
thousand camels'.

Territories whose monarchs had been invited to accept Islam but refused
were counted as part of the *Dar al-Harb*, the 'region of war' where conflict
might justly be imposed until those who dissented became Muslim or
formally submitted and became *dhimmi*. Nowhere was this rule applied for
longer than the border with the Byzantine Empire. The buffer zone running
the length of the Taurus Mountains was known to the Arabs as *al-dāwahī*,
'the outer lands'. The Arab side of the frontier was dubbed *al-thughūr*,
'the passageways', behind which lay an intermediate zone of towns and
strongholds known as the *'awāsim*, the 'protectresses'. The Arab military
presence was centred on the *amsar*, garrison towns, along the frontier. Abu
Yusuf's *Kitāb al-Kharāj*, dating from the caliphate of Harun al-Rashid,
describes these as 'the prop of Islam, the bane of the enemy and the gatherers
of wealth'.

By the time of the great expedition against Constantinople, Arab armies
had experienced generations of almost unbroken success, and expectations

Constantinople's century of sieges, 626–718

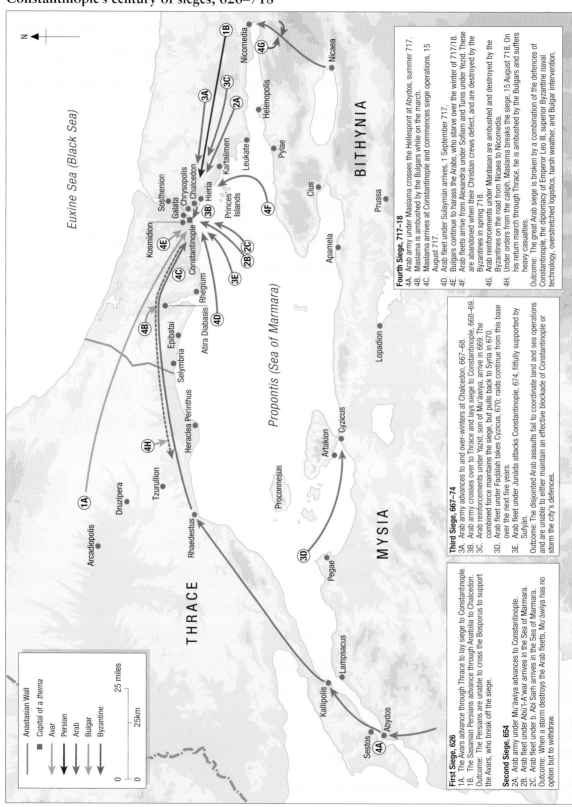

Euxine Sea (Black Sea)

BITHYNIA

MYSIA

THRACE

Propontis (Sea of Marmara)

N

Nicomedia
Nicaea
Helenopolis
Pylae
Leukate
Kartalimen
Cius
Sosthenion
Chrysopolis
Galata
Chalcedon
Hieria
Princes'
Islands
Kosmidion
Apamela
Constantinople
Prussa
Rhegium
Atira Diabasis
Epibatai
Selymbria
Heraclea Perinthus
Lopadion
Proconnesus
Artakion
Cyzicus
Pegae
Rhaedestus
Tzurullion
Druzipera
Arcadiopolis
Lampsacus
Kallipolis
Sestos
Abydos

Legend:
- Anastasian Wall
- Capital of a *thema*
- Avar
- Persian
- Arab
- Bulgar
- Byzantine

0 — 25 miles
0 — 25km

First Siege, 626
1A. The Avars advance through Thrace to lay siege to Constantinople.
1B. The Sasanian Persians advance through Anatolia to Chalcedon.
Outcome: The Persians are unable to cross the Bosporus to support the Avars, who break off the siege.

Second Siege, 654
2A. Arab army under Muʿāwiya advances to Constantinople.
2B. Arab fleet under Abū'l-Aʿwar arrives in the Sea of Marmara.
2C. Arab fleet under b. Abī Sarh arrives in the Sea of Marmara.
Outcome: When a storm destroys the Arab fleets, Muʿāwiya has no option but to withdraw.

Third Siege, 667–74
3A. Arab army advances to and over-winters at Chalcedon, 667–68.
3B. Arab army crosses over to Thrace and lays siege to Constantinople, 668–69.
3C. Arab reinforcements under Yazīd, son of Muʿāwiya, arrive in 669. The combined force maintains the siege, but pulls back to Syria in 670.
3D. Arab fleet under Fadāla takes Cyzicus, 670; raids continue from this base over the next five years.
3E. Arab fleet under Junāda attacks Constantinople, 674, fitfully supported by Sufyān.
Outcome: The disjointed Arab assaults fail to coordinate land and sea operations and are unable to either maintain an effective blockade of Constantinople or storm the city's defences.

Fourth Siege, 717–18
4A. Arab army under Maslama crosses the Hellespont at Abydos, summer 717.
4B. Maslama is ambushed by the Bulgars while on the march.
4C. Maslama arrives at Constantinople and commences siege operations, 15 August 717.
4D. Arab fleet under Sulaymān arrives, 1 September 717.
4E. Bulgars continue to harass the Arabs, who starve over the winter of 717/18.
4F. Arab fleets arrive from Alexandria under Sofiam and Tunis under Yezid. These are abandoned when their Christian crews defect, and are destroyed by the Byzantines in spring 718.
4G. Arab reinforcements under Mardasan are ambushed and destroyed by the Byzantines on the road from Nicaea to Nicomedia.
4H. Under orders from the caliph, Maslama breaks the siege, 15 August 718. On his return march through Thrace, he is ambushed by the Bulgars and suffers heavy casualties.
Outcome: The great Arab siege is broken by a combination of the defences of Constantinople, the diplomacy of Emperor Leo III, superior Byzantine naval technology, overstretched logistics, harsh weather, and Bulgar intervention.

were high that this next phase would represent the crowning glory of Islamic arms. The verses of 'Amr b. Kulthum reflect this triumphalism:

> Bite we sharp with our swords, nor apportion mercy …
> Not a babe of ours but shall win to manhood,
> Find the world at his knees, its great ones kneeling.

BYZANTINE

Byzantine history commands little interest and less respect in the West. 'A worthless repertory of declamations and miracles,' wrote Voltaire; 'a disgrace to the human mind'. Montesquieu dismissed it as 'nothing more than a tissue of revolts, seditions, and perfidies'. Hegel considered it 'a disgusting picture of imbecility,' governed by an ethos alien to 'the growth of all that is noble in thoughts, deeds, and persons'.

While philosophers could talk around the subject, historians had no option but to address it. Edward Gibbon lamented having to account for this 'distressful period, when the degenerate Romans of the East were incapable of contending with the warlike enthusiasm and youthful vigour of the Saracens'. All he could discern from the Byzantine military record were the 'lifeless hands' and 'languid souls' of an 'unwarlike people'. This bias, deep-rooted in dogmatic prejudices that stretch back to Europe's Dark Ages, is as untrue as it is unfair. In reality, no empire in history survived losing so many battles and so much territory in so short a time. For more than 300 years – from the usurpation of Phocas in 602 until the reign of Romanos I Lekapenos and the campaigns of his great general John Kourkouas in the 10th century – Byzantine territory and culture were effectively under permanent siege from a host of enemies, east and west: Persians, Avars, Arabs, Bulgars, Magyars, and Rus'. The term 'byzantine' is synonymous with bureaucracy, treachery, and administration by eunuchs and 'women surrendering themselves to lusts and abominations of all kinds', as Hegel labelled them. But the fact the Byzantine state could survive the maelstrom of violence it was subjected to is testament to the professionalism of its military infrastructure and inherent toughness of its fighting men.

The continuity of imperial military doctrine was reflected in the texts authored by the emperors themselves, from the 6th-century *Strategikon* of Maurice to the late 9th-century/early 10th-century *Taktika* of Leo VI. Maurice had advised seeking victory via 'stratagems rather than by sheer force'. Be prepared to negotiate in bad faith with the foe to buy time; set an ambush on his route of march; look to foment treason within his ranks, and seek allies in his rear and on his flanks. Always undertake a scorched earth policy as the enemy advances, for 'the general achieves the most who tries to destroy the enemy's army more by hunger than by force of arms'. In all things, be ready; whatever the outcome, 'a general should never have the excuse, "I did not expect it."'

This painting from the *katholikon* (main church) of the monastery of Hosios Loukas, a UNESCO World Heritage Site near Distomo in Boeotia, Greece, illustrates the Biblical Patriarch Joshua's encounter with the captain of the hosts of the Lord. It in fact represents the heavy infantry of the contemporary Byzantine Empire. Note in particular the lamellar armour worn over a coat of chainmail that extends from the neck to the wrists. (akg-images/Paul Ancenay)

Because of this institutional professionalism, as the early 10th-century Iraqi administrator and geographer Qudāma b. Ja'far warned, 'it behoves the Muslims to be most wary and on their guard against the Rūm, from amongst all the ranks of their adversaries'.

Nevertheless, the initial onslaught of Islam had pushed the imperial war machine to the brink of complete collapse. The Arab jihad permanently divested Constantinople of her richest provinces, Egypt, Syria and Africa; by the end of the 7th century, total annual imperial revenue had collapsed to perhaps 20 per cent of the level prior to the invasions. As just one example of the systemic shocks the Byzantine military was subjected to, at the end of the 6th century arms and armour were a state monopoly produced in *armamenton* (arsenals) established in major cities such as Alexandria, Antioch, and Damascus. All three of these were in Arab hands less than 50 years later.

Urban centres in what was left of the empire contracted or disappeared during the 7th and 8th centuries, marking the end of a way of life that had defined classical Mediterranean culture for more than a thousand years. 'In the days of old, cities were numerous in Rūm but now they have become few,' wrote the anonymous author of the 10th-century *Hudūd al-'Alām*. Trade collapsed, and as coinage declined in circulation, barter replaced currency as the principal means of exchange, a transition marked by the shift in agricultural production from cash crops (olives, grapes) to grains (wheat, barley) in Anatolia. Byzantine society devolved into rural communities centred on fortified redoubts, and imperial armies were forced to evolve accordingly. During the reign of Maurice, the Byzantine armed forces consisted of seven *exerciti*, field armies each commanded by a *magister militium*. These consisted of the Exerciti Orientalis in Syria, Palestine, Cilicia, and Mesopotamia; Exerciti Ilyricum and Thracianus in the western and eastern Balkans respectively; Exerciti Africam, Italiae and Armeniam in Africa, Italy, and Armenia respectively; and the Obsequium, formed from the troops formerly attached to the Magistri Militum Praesentales, stationed in north-western Anatolia and usually under the emperor himself.

With manpower and revenues in freefall during the 7th century, the emperors Heraclius, Constans II, and Constantine IV had to radically reform what was left of the military in order to establish a line of defence along the Taurus Mountains and hold on to Asia Minor, the last remaining contiguous bloc of land within the empire. This expedient evolved into the system of territorial Themes, within which local field commanders were expected to operate as autonomously and self-sufficiently as possible. Eventually, these units gave their name to the provinces where they settled, and the term 'theme' came to mean not only the military unit but also the administrative division in which it settled.

The armies of the two Magistri Militum Praesentales in north-western Asia Minor and the shrunken remnant of Thrace were dubbed the Opsikion Theme. The forces of the Magister Militum per Orientum were renamed the Anatolikan Theme and settled in the southern part of Asia Minor, stretching from Cappadocia in the east to Lycia in the west, with its northern and southern boundaries defined by the Halys River valley and the Taurus Mountains, respectively. The army of the Magister Militum per Armeniam became the Armeniakon Theme covering the northern and eastern provinces

of Asia Minor. The forces of the Magister Militum per Thracias were resettled in west-central Asia Minor as the Thracesion Theme. The Aegean islands and the scattered outposts clinging to the coastline where the empire still retained authority were incorporated into the maritime Karabision Theme, initially headquartered on the island of Rhodes.

Supreme military authority in each Theme was invested in the *stratêgos*, appointed directly by Constantinople. State supply depots (*apothêkai*) were established in the Themes. Constantinople remained connected to the Taurus frontier via the great trunk road that ran from Chrysopolis on the Asian shore of the Bosporus to Ancyra and thence either directly east across Galatia or south-east through Cappadocia.

The thematic armies were organized into units called *tourmai*, *droungoi*, and *banda* – very roughly, divisions, brigades, and regiments. While the middle level of this structure always remained a tactical unit and was not tied to a specific locale, the first and last of these had a definitive territorial identity. Local defence was organized around the basic administrative and military unit, the *bandon*, under a *komēs*. Each *bandon* was identified with a clearly defined community, from which it drew its ranks. Two to five *banda* made up a *droungoi*, commanded by a *droungarios*. Three *droungoi* formed a *tourma* centred on a headquarters fortress or fortified town, where the commanding officer (the *tourmaches*) was charged with maintaining the strongpoints under his authority, as well as the safety and property of the local population. It was his responsibility to suppress minor raids into his territory, shadow major incursions, provide the imperial field army with reconnaissance and other intelligence, and stage raids and ambushes where possible. Under an

The Taurus Mountain range runs roughly north-east across Anatolia from the Mediterranean to the Black Sea. According to John Julius Norwich, in the 6th–7th centuries, imperial defences here represented 'the front line of Christendom, on whose integrity and inviolability all Europe depended'. The Taurus Mountains represented a physical as well as political boundary between the caliphate and the empire. The winter weather on the Anatolian plateau was not congenial for Arab *razzias*. 'Often while making their incursions and plundering raids at such times, they have been overcome by the Romans and destroyed,' emperor Leo VI noted in his *Taktika*. From an Arab perspective, the 10th-century geographer Qudāma b. Ja'far recommended that winter expeditions into Byzantine territory should not last longer than 20 days. (h4bib/Pixabay)

The men of the thematic units received a salary (*roga*), were entitled to a percentage of any loot, and could expect a periodic bonus (*doreai*) corresponding to a special event, such as the accession of a new emperor. Military landholdings (*stratiôtika ktêmata*) that could be passed on to their heirs in exchange for service to the state were awarded to soldiers of the thematic armies. However, it was not necessary that the owner of the land offer himself for military service; he could pay someone else to serve in his place, on condition that he also covered all expenses for equipment and subsistence (*syndosis*). The military service corresponding to a plot of land could be shared between various owners. Under no circumstances could they be exempted from the obligation of offering the owed service except when the land was sold or donated, in which case the military service obligation was transferred to the new owner.

This system constituted the backbone of the Byzantine state because it created a landed peasantry determined to stand its ground, fight, and rebuild in order to preserve and pass on what was theirs. It created a bond between the emperors and their rank and file because, in exchange for their service, the common people were offered protection by the state from predatory private interests. Seen in this light, iconoclasm was in many ways a reaction against the disproportionate, and growing, influence of the monasteries. These sometimes allied with the aristocracy (*dynatoi*), who were always seeking to expropriate the smallholders in order to build up the power of their great houses at the expense of central authority. The emperors were constantly struggling to face down this internal threat, as epitomized in the tax increases and agrarian reform legislation sponsored by Romanus I Lekapenos in 934:

A clash between Byzantine and Arab cavalry, as depicted in a stylized representation in the *Madrid Skylitzes*. Byzantine cavalry of this era rode into battle armed with a recurve composite bow of the Hunnic style, a quiver of 30–40 arrows, two long spears, and a long sword. Armour included a hooded coat of chainmail, a plumed iron helmet, and iron gauntlets. This combination allowed for a versatile combatant, well adapted for ranged and close combat according to tactical need. The professionalism of the Byzantine military establishment made it the most enduring of the caliphate's foes. (Album/akg-images)

This interesting ivory carving representation of a 7th-century Byzantine emperor, probably Heraclius, depicts him bearing a small, circular shield and wielding a short sword. Heraclius was the first emperor to lead the imperial army in person since Theodosius I at the end of the 4th century, so grave was the strategic situation at the time of his accession in 610. It was a calculated risk; should an emperor take the field and suffer defeat, his authority might be fatally undermined. Conversely, delegating responsibility to a victorious subordinate might create a dangerous rival. (The Walters Museum)

'It is not through hatred and envy of the rich that we take these measures, but for the protection of the small and the safety of the empire as a whole … The extension of the power of the strong … will bring about the irreparable loss of the public good, if the present law does not bring a check to it. For it is the many, settled on the land, who provide for the general needs, who pay the taxes and furnish the army with recruits. Everything fails when the many are wanting.'

These issues would have struck Leo III as singularly academic in the summer of 717, as the host of Maslama closed in on Constantinople. As emperor he would have been accompanied by his guard Hetaereia cavalry and Numeri infantry, but the thematic troops he led on campaign against Theodosius III would have returned to their posts once he was enthroned, for he could not leave the provinces unmanned: if Leo committed all of the imperial field armies to the defence of the capital, the Arabs would annex Asia Minor by default. The active defence of Constantinople would therefore have been undertaken by a very heterogeneous mix of available units.

In peacetime, order was maintained by the urban Watch (Kerketon) under the prefect of the city. Constantinople did not possess a standing urban militia, but the city's trade associations or guilds could be called upon in times of crisis. Each of these corporations (*systêmata*), from butchers to jewellers, had a duty to man a particular stretch of wall. The political factions (*demes*) of the Blues and Greens could also be mobilized.

πεπ ηκ(ων). Ηρωσδὲ καὶ τὸ σκλαγῳπρ πολὸ ωῖπυρὶ

φολεφωπολ πυρπολ   τον τωνι ΗΛΗΠφλον

Greek Fire in action, from the *Madrid Skylitzes*. Marcus Graecus, a writer of the 10th century, listed its chemical components: 'Take pure sulphur, tartar, saracolla [Persian gum], pitch, dissolved nitre, petroleum and pine resin; boil these together, then saturate tow with the result and set fire to it. The conflagration will spread, and can be extinguished only by urine, vinegar or sand.' (Public domain)

Other than the regiments manning the walls, regular troops stationed in the capital included the palace guard (Noumera), mercenaries (*foederati*), and the personal security details (*bucellarii*) of the highest-ranking civil and military officers. Other detachments on hand included the Scholae, Candidati, Domestici, and Excubitores, but these once elite guards units had degenerated into little more than ceremonial parade ground formations. More useful were the Spatharii, comprised of promising young officers being trained for higher rank. Finally, while dedicated to securing the waters around the city, the marines of the imperial navy could be committed to fighting for the land walls if the struggle there ever hung in the balance.

Having mentioned its nautical component, no discussion of the Byzantine military would be complete without reference to its signature weapon: Greek Fire (a term coined by Latins from the west during the Crusades; the Byzantines themselves called it by several names, including 'marine fire', 'liquid fire', 'prepared fire', and 'artificial fire'). Incendiary compounds have a certain lineage in antiquity, being described in Philostratus's *Life of Apollonius* and Vegetius's *De Re Militari*. But none of these were effectively weaponized until the 7th century when, according to Theophanes, Kallinikios, a Christian refugee from Heliopolis in Syria, arrived in Constantinople and 'manufactured a naval fire with which he kindled the ships of the Arabs and burnt them with their crews'. The effects were horrific. Like napalm, Greek Fire clung to everything it touched, and the flames could not be doused with water; men, burning alive, would find no relief even by hurling themselves into the sea.

However, while Greek Fire was a critical asset in the right circumstances, it was not actually divine intervention. It was only viable in specific environments – the close waters of the Bosporus were ideal – with the right winds and tides. It was not risked in offensive actions, and was reserved for the imperial navy, being denied to the thematic fleets for fear of rebellion.

THE SIEGE OF CONSTANTINOPLE, 717–18

The caliph al-Walīd was planning a grand expedition against Constantinople when he died in Damascus on 23 February 715, after a reign of ten years. He left behind 19 sons, but it was his brother, Sulaymān b. al-Malik, who was acclaimed caliph at Ramla, in Palestine, that same day.

It was an auspicious time, as the armies of the faithful were proving invincible on all fronts, and the advance of the caliphate appeared irresistible. In the east, Qutaybah b. Muslim had crossed the Oxus and seized Bukhara in 709. The following year – with the inducement 'you are governor over whatever lands you conquer' – Muḥammad b. Qāsim subjugated Sind, bringing the Arab frontier to the Indus River. In 712, Qutaybah b. Muslim took Samarqand, advanced to the Jaxartes, and occupied Ferghana, bringing the caliphate to the borders of T'ang dynasty China.

Progress was equally dramatic to the west. In 702, Marwān instructed his brother, 'Umar b. al-'Aziz, governor of Egypt, to appoint Musa b. Nusayr governor of Ifriqiyah and send a thousand Coptic shipwrights with him to construct a fleet at the new regional capital, Tunis. 'He ordered him to impose on the Berbers the perpetual duty of having to bring to the dockyard by the strength of their arms the wood necessary to build ships, given that he would have to have a fleet equipped there, in order to fight the Rūm on land and at sea and carry out raids on the coastline of their country.' This projection of Arab naval power exposed all the islands of the Mediterranean to raids. In the spring of 710, Arab forces took the city of Tangier, completing the conquest of North Africa. In 711, Ṭāriq b. Ziyād crossed the Pillars of Hercules (the Rock would ever after bear his name as Jabal Ṭāriq – 'Ṭāriq's Mount' – which evolved into Gibraltar) and defeated the Visigoth King Roderic at the Battle of Guadalete, setting in motion the conquest of Hispania (al-Andalus) and the advance to the Pyrenees.

In this increasingly millenarian atmosphere, signs and portents of impending triumph were readily available. In the Muslim calendar, the year 100 was fast approaching. According to the *Kitāb al-'Uyun*, Sulaymān 'was informed by many learned men that the name of the caliph who should take Kustantiniyyah (Constantinople) should be the name of a prophet'. Sulaymān – i.e. Solomon – seized on this mandate as his duty and his destiny as spiritual and political head of the *ummah*; 'he was eagerly desirous of doing it and made preparations for this purpose, never doubting that it was he who should perform this'. Caught up in the triumphalist mood of the era, the new caliph ordered the mobilization

A silver dirham of the Umayyad caliph Sulaymān b. al-Malik (r. 715–17), instigator of the great campaign against Constantinople. The Arab chronicler b. Wāḍiḥ al-Ya'qūbī described him as tall, 'attractive and eloquent' but notoriously 'a voracious eater who was rarely satiated … with a body that could not bear hunger'. He is alleged to have eaten in one sitting a whole lamb, six chickens, 70 pomegranates, and a basket of currants. In spite of this gluttony, he took an active interest in military matters, was determined to take Constantinople, and died in camp at Dabiq with his army. (Noble Numismatics, https://www.noble.com.au/)

The Cilician Gates, a critical chokepoint in the Taurus Mountains frontier between the empire and the caliphate. There were only three passes large enough to allow ingress and egress to an army on campaign. The pass from Cilicia went north through the Taurus Mountains towards Karaman, Konya, and Kayseri; that from Adana, north through the Anti-Taurus Mountains towards Kayseri, Ankara, and the Black Sea; and that from Malatya, either west through the Anti-Taurus Mountains to Kayseri, or north-west to Sivas, or north along the upper Euphrates valley towards Trebizond. The Byzantines rarely tried to block these routes for fear of being outflanked, normally attacking Muslim raiders as they returned home laden with booty. In response, the Muslims often entered Byzantine territory by one pass and left via another, which demanded considerable logistical forethought. (The Library of Congress)

of the entire Umayyad war machine, pledging, 'I shall not cease from the struggle with Constantinople until either I conquer it or I destroy the entire dominion of the Arabs in trying.'

As for the Byzantines, by contrast, 'their days were days of confusion and disorder,' the *Kitāb al-'Uyun* concluded. The emperors, who once held sway from Carthage to the Caucasus, now reigned over little more than Asia Minor, and much of this remaining asset had been reduced to a wasteland after decades of incessant Arab incursions. 'You might see the world brought back to its ancient silence; no voice in the field,' wrote the 8th-century chronicler Paul the Deacon: 'Human habitations had become places of refuge for wild beasts.' The empire was trapped in a vicious downward spiral. The collapse in trade, manpower, and agricultural yields across its heartland dragged tax revenue down with it; the shrunken imperial treasury could not meet the demand for armies and fleets to protect the frontiers; the heartland was thus exposed to further depredation.

Much of this trauma, however, was self-inflicted. 'On account of the frequent assumptions of imperial power and the prevalence of usurpation, the affairs of the empire and of the City were being neglected and declined,' Nicephorus noted. What was left of the empire seemed to be descending into anarchy; six emperors had now ascended the throne in just 20 years, and five of those reigns had ended violently. 'As a result, the enemy were able to overrun the Roman state with impunity and cause much slaughter, abduction and the capture of cities. For this reason also the Saracens advanced on the imperial city itself, sending forth by land an innumerable host of horse and foot from the various peoples subject to them, as well as a great fleet.'

It was Sulaymān's son, Dawūd, who led the summer campaign against the Byzantine frontier, capturing Hisn al-Mar'a ('The Woman's Fortress') that guarded the approaches to Melitene. This northern *razzia* may have been intended as a feint, for the vanguard of the main Umayyad invasion force, under Sulaymān b. Mu'ad and Bakhtari b. al-Hasan, entered Asia Minor to the south via the Cilician Gates, taking the strategic fortress of Loulon on the way, and wintering in a fortified camp (*khandaq*) on Byzantine territory. In early 716, Sulaymān's army continued into central Asia Minor. The Umayyad fleet under 'Umar b. Hubayra al-Fazārī cruised along the Anatolian coast, while Maslama 'marched behind them with a great deal of military equipment'. Maslama's key subordinates included the commanders (*wujūh*) of the caliphate's elite Syrian units (*ahl al-shām*), 'Abd Allāh b. Abī Zakariyyā al-Khuzā'ī, Muḥammad b. Jabr, and Khālid b. Ma'dan (who had a highly personal stake in the campaign, given he was the promulgator of Hadith 4:175, 'The first army from amongst my followers who conquers the city of Caesar will be forgiven their sins').

The total strength of the Umayyad host was reported as 'innumerable' by the late 8th-century *Zuqnin Chronicle*. More constructively, the 9th-century account of Theophanes mentions 1,800 ships, while the 10th-century Arab writer al-Mas'udi references 120,000 troops. According to the *Chronicle of 1234*, Sulaymān 'mustered an army of 200,000 and built 5,000 ships, which he filled with troops and provisions'. The supply train alone is said to have numbered 12,000 men, 6,000 camels, and 6,000 donkeys. Complementing the regular forces, 3,000 volunteers (*muttawi'ah*), 'the class of Arabs without possessions', signed up for the campaign in the hope of gaining divine credit and earthly spoils. Arab financiers provided mounts for the troops on the basis of hire or sale in the expectation of being recompensed from the booty to be extracted from the imperial city.

The Belgrade Gate (the Byzantine Second Military Gate) at Constantinople, flanked by towers 22 and 23. Expectations in the Islamic world that the fall of Constantinople was imminent were raised to fever pitch in 716 (98 AH) as the massed land and naval forces of the faithful were unleashed by the caliph Sulaymān. The imperial enemy had been ruthlessly chipped away at for decades by a relentless sequence of *razzias* (raids) that had driven the Byzantine state to its knees. All that was required was one last thrust directly at its heart and the empire would finally collapse. (Author's collection)

AMBUSH OF AN ARAB PATROL (PP. 52–53)

In spring 716, the largest army ever assembled by the Umayyad caliphate traversed the passes of the Taurus Mountains (**1**) and entered the territory of the Byzantine Empire. Its objective was Constantinople. This host of infantry, horse and camel cavalry, siege machines, and a vast baggage train (**2**) under the command of Maslama b. 'Abd al-Malik, half-brother of Caliph Sulaymān b. 'Abd al-Malik, would march unhindered across the Anatolian plateau to the gates of the imperial capital itself.

The Byzantines had been contesting this frontier with the Arabs for decades in a strategy based on defence in depth. If at all possible, Arab incursions were to be held and turned back at the line of the Taurus Mountains by locally based units called *kleisourarchies*, who were charged with monitoring the passes (*kleisouraí*) habitually exploited by raiders. A local military aristocracy, the *akrites* (from the Greek word *akrai*, meaning fringes, or borders) emerged in these regions, constructing their own fortresses, living off revenue from fighting the Arabs, and maintaining relative autonomy from Constantinople.

If an Arab force was too strong to be held at this line (which was frequently the case), the *akrites* were expected to evacuate those villagers and livestock in the path of the invasion while continuing to shadow and harass the intruders, making sure to track and report their movements to the professional troops of the Thematic armies as these converged on the scene.

But the Byzantine field armies could do nothing to prevent this Umayyad juggernaut – obscured by the great clouds of dust kicked up by tens of thousands of tramping feet, hooves, and wheels – from penetrating into the heartland of their empire. Their only recourse was observation and identifying targets of opportunity, such as the outriding patrol (**3**) drawing close to where a cluster of Byzantine troops are preparing an ambush.

The troops reflect a heterogeneous mix of uniform types, symptomatic of an era where the transition from a late-Roman to a definitively Byzantine style was in process. While a heavy infantry soldier keeps watch (**4**), an officer (**5**) is instructing a mounted dispatch rider (**6**) to circulate his order that the other teams of observers scattered about are to converge on this location. Waiting patiently for the opportune moment are a horse archer (**7**) and a representative from the 'emperor's hammer', the Byzantine heavy cavalry, a cataphract (**8**).

The walkway surmounting the inner wall at Constantinople was wide enough to accommodate one file of troops manning the battlements while allowing another file to move north or south unobstructed behind them. It was not wide enough to support artillery, which was concentrated in the towers. (Author's collection)

The Byzantines, consumed with their own internecine strife, were in no position to check this juggernaut even had they desired to do so. Leo, the *stratêgos* of the Anatolikan Theme, had remained loyal to Anastasius II and never recognized the ascension of Theodosius III. He was covertly in collusion with Artabasdos, the *stratêgos* of the Armeniakon Theme, and was simultaneously in communication with Maslama, creating the impression he would sell out the empire in exchange for serving as the Umayyad puppet emperor in the aftermath upon the fall of Constantinople. According to the *Kitāb al-'Uyun*, Maslama 'came to terms with him and gave him security', in exchange for which Leo 'should give him advice and information for attacking the people of Kustantiniyyah'. Maslama was playing a double game here because, according to Agapius, Anastasius II had also 'sent messengers to Maslama', requesting him to ask Sulaymān for support in retaining his throne.

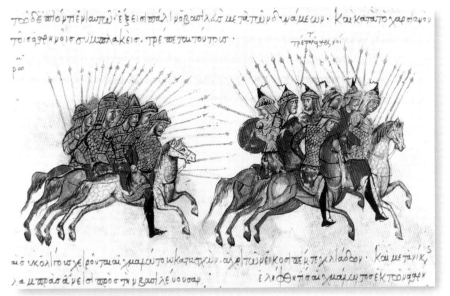

A stylized representation of a battle between the Byzantines and the Arabs from the *Madrid Skylitzes*. The Byzantine cavalry on the left are noticeably more heavily armoured than their Arab counterparts, but this still does not extend to the horses, which are depicted unprotected. By the 10th century, the mounts of the Byzantine cataphract heavy cavalry were completely encased in a coat of armour that reached down to their hoofs. This created the eerie effect of them moving without seeming to have legs as they charged. (Album/akg-images)

Sulaymān advanced to Amorium, the capital of the Anatolikan Theme, which had closed its gates to Leo because it had declared for Theodosius III. Sulaymān could have stormed the city, but he wanted it intact to use as a base to wait out the following winter, and saw it as an opportunity to bolster Leo's position as a counterweight to Theodosius III. From outside the walls of the city, Sulaymān's troops were ordered to shout, 'Long live the emperor Leo!' and to encourage the city's defenders to take up the cry. They offered the city terms of surrender if its inhabitants would acknowledge Leo as emperor.

Leo arrived with a personal guard of 300 cavalry and camped a half-mile from the besieging Arabs. Three days of negotiation ensued, in bad faith on both sides. Sulaymān set an ambush for Leo, but the *stratêgos* slipped away. Frustrated by this inactivity, Sulaymān's 'emirs and army rebelled against him', asking, '"Why are we besieging walls instead of raiding?" They struck their tents and withdrew.'

Michael the Syrian asserts the citizens of Amorium were still reluctant to accept Leo's authority because accounts of his dealings with the Arabs were public knowledge. According to the *Kitāb al-ʿUyun*, Leo won them over by assuring them:

> I will not rule over you except by your commands; but you have heard of my character and my valour and ability, and your affairs are in confusion, and your kingdom is sore smitten, and the civil war is raging, and this Maslama, the son of ʿAbd al-Malik, has come close to your territory, and he will attack you. Therefore, let me in and entrust your government to me; and, if I bear myself in it in accordance with your wishes, well; but if not, turn me out and do with me what you please.

The defences of Constantinople, looking north on a restored section of the outer wall with the inner wall to the right. The terrace between the inner and outer walls, dubbed the *peribolos*, was between 15m and 19.5m wide. The inner wall rises some 9.3m above the present exterior ground level and approximately 12.2m above the ground level within the city, with battlements 1.4m high running the length of the outward facing side. The thickness of the inner wall ranges from 4.7m at the base to 4.15m at the top. Note how the tower on the inner wall looms over the battlements of the outer. Most of the defenders of the city would have been assigned posts along the outer wall, supported by archers and artillery stationed in the towers of the inner wall. (Author's collection)

Leo swore 'he would break faith with Maslama and renounce him and fight against him; and he said to them, "You know my valour and prowess in war and my military capacities, and you know his ways and his soft character, and I can obtain from him whatever I wish."' Leo was able to install an 800-man garrison in Amorium, evacuating the non-combatants as he withdrew to Pisidia. In summer, supported by Artabasdos, he was proclaimed and crowned as Byzantine emperor, making his repudiation of Theodosius III overt.

Maslama was with the main Arab army, which assembled at Dabiq and then marched north through Germanicia to cross the Taurus Mountains, where he occupied Cappadocia without resistance. Leo continued to string him along, sending envoys to his camp near Masalaion to assure him, 'I have received your letters and accept your plan. Behold, I am on my way to you.' Convinced Leo and Artabasdos were his for the taking, Maslama did not devastate the territories of the Armeniakon and Anatolikan Themes as he marched through them, issuing orders that his men were forbidden to plunder those territories, 'not even taking a loaf of bread'. Leo, in turn, commanded that a travelling market should be loaded up for the Arabs, and the Byzantines bought and sold in good faith and without fear.

According to the *Kitāb al-ʿUyun*, Maslama reasoned he had nothing to lose by backing one side in an incipient Byzantine civil war. If Leo's bid to claim the throne failed, it would still fatally undermine the empire's capacity to resist the oncoming Umayyad onslaught. If he won, he would have no choice but to surrender Constantinople and accept subordinate status as a puppet emperor, because he would be too tainted by his association with the Arabs for the people to rally behind him if he attempted to rule in his own right. Maslama could – and later did – let it be known that Leo allowed himself to be considered Maslama's *mawla*, or client. However, Leo kept finding excuses not to arrive and pledge his fealty in person. Maslama was suspicious; at Theodosiana he told the envoys, 'I see your general is playing with me'.

'Heaven forbid!' they replied. But Maslama, who could not remain in temporary camps with so large an army, moved on to Akroinon and from there to the Aegean coast, sacking Sardis and Pergamum en route. 'Many cities in the region of Asia fell to them that summer,' the *Chronicle of 1234* records, 'and they ruined them and took captives and looted, slaughtering the men and sending the children and women back as slaves to their own country'. Maslama sent Sulaymān ahead with 12,000 men to invest Chalcedon, 'to cut off supplies from that approach to Constantinople and to lay waste and pillage Roman territory in general'. The Arab fleet meanwhile wintered in Cilicia.

For centuries, the Golden Gate was where the emperors would return to Constantinople celebrating a triumph over their enemies. Emperors also entered the city upon being elevated to the throne, as in the case of Nicephorus II in 963. Official delegations to the emperor, such as papal legates in 519 and 868 and Pope Constantine himself in 710, were also welcomed at the Golden Gate. The gate was bricked up long before the final fall of the city to Ottoman Turks in 1453. (Author's collection)

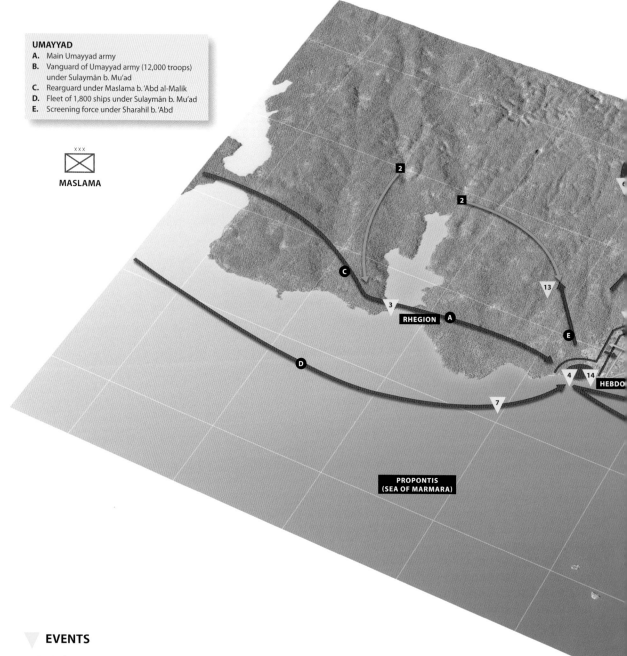

UMAYYAD
- **A.** Main Umayyad army
- **B.** Vanguard of Umayyad army (12,000 troops) under Sulaymān b. Mu'ad
- **C.** Rearguard under Maslama b. 'Abd al-Malik
- **D.** Fleet of 1,800 ships under Sulaymān b. Mu'ad
- **E.** Screening force under Sharahil b. 'Abd

XXX
MASLAMA

2

2

13

C

3

RHEGION **A**

E

D

4 **14**

HEBDO

7

**PROPONTIS
(SEA OF MARMARA)**

▼ EVENTS

1. 25 March 717: Having marched to Chrysopolis and opened negotiations with the Patriarch and Senate of Constantinople, the Byzantine usurper Konon forces the abdication of the emperor Theodosius III and his own coronation as Leo III.

2. Summer, 717: A 12,000-strong Umayyad vanguard under Sulaymān b. Mu'ad advances to Chalcedon.

3. June: After crossing the Hellespont at Abydos, the main Umayyad army marches on Constantinople. The 4,000-strong caliphal rearguard under the personal command of Maslama b. 'Abd al-Malik has to fight its way through a Bulgar ambush.

4. 15 August: The Umayyad army arrives under the walls of Constantinople, sets up camp at the Hebdomon, and establishes siege lines.

5. Late August: The Umayyad army's attempt to storm the land walls of Constantinople fails.

6. Late August: Maslama sends out detachments to plunder the countryside and eliminate any outlying Byzantine garrisons.

7. 1 September: The Umayyad fleet of 1,800 ships under Sulaymān b. Mu'ad arrives.

8. 3 September: The Umayyad fleet splits into two detachments. The southern wing anchors at Eutropius and Anthemios, the harbours of Chalcedon.

9. 3 September: As the northern wing of the Umayyad fleet transits up the Bosporus, it is ambushed by imperial dromons using Greek Fire.

10. 3 September: The 20 transport ships at the tail of the Umayyad fleet are destroyed; some sink, some crash against the sea walls of Constantinople, and the wrecks of some ships, still burning, drift as far south as the Princes' Islands.

11. 4 September: The Umayyad fleet's northern wing anchors at Kleidion and Sosthenion.

12. Autumn: Naval encounters at sea and clashes along the land walls play out on a daily basis, as Maslama and Sulaymān b. Mu'ad seek to tighten their cordon around Constantinople, while Leo III continues to probe the perimeter of their blockade.

13. Autumn: In a major battle, the Bulgars inflict considerable losses on the Umayyad screening force under Sharahil b. 'Abd.

14. 8 October: Death of Sulaymān b. Mu'ad.

15. Winter: Freezing weather descends on the Umayyad siege lines; snow blankets the ground well into the new year. Starving and sick, the besiegers are vulnerable to sorties by the imperial garrison.

CONSTANTINOPLE, 717

The events around Constantinople, summer–winter, 717

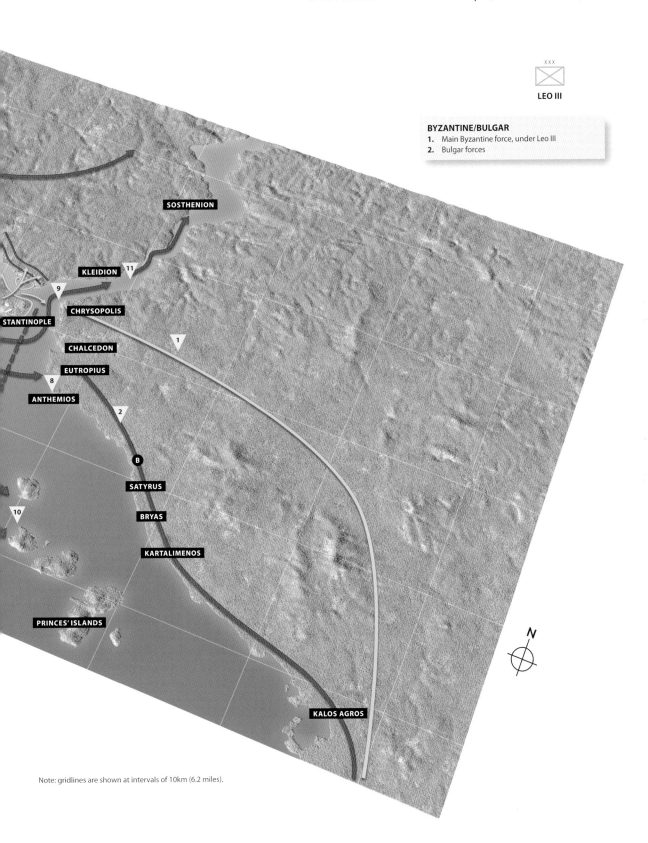

XXX

LEO III

BYZANTINE/BULGAR
1. Main Byzantine force, under Leo III
2. Bulgar forces

SOSTHENION

KLEIDION 11

9

CHRYSOPOLIS

STANTINOPLE

CHALCEDON

1

EUTROPIUS

8

ANTHEMIOS

2

B

SATYRUS

10

BRYAS

KARTALIMENOS

PRINCES' ISLANDS

N

KALOS AGROS

Note: gridlines are shown at intervals of 10km (6.2 miles).

Four Ottoman minarets now surround Hagia Sophia. According to the earliest Arab narrative of the siege, the Umayyad commander Maslama wrote to Leo: 'I declare to thee that I have committed myself by oath not to return to my native country before I have broken thy empire, pulled down the fortifications of this capital in which thou puttest all thy trust, made, out of the place of thy cult, the basilica of Saint Sophia, a bathhouse for my troops, and broken upon thy head the wood of the cross which thou adorest.' (Author's collection)

The caliph Sulaymān played no further role in the campaign. He had remained with the reserve army at Dabiq in preparation for the march the following spring to link up with the advance force at Constantinople. If Maslama had already taken the city, Sulaymān would inherit the triumph. If the siege were ongoing, his reinforcements would provide the final impetus to victory. But it was not to be, as Sulaymān died suddenly on 24 September 717.

Before he expired, the caliph consulted with his advisors as to the succession. His son Dawūd was on campaign with Maslama. Were he named heir, a long interregnum would take place before he returned to Damascus, and civil war might ensue. His second son was too young. The compromise choice was his cousin and closest confidant, 'Umar b. al-'Aziz, with the stipulation his successor would be Sulaymān's brother Yazīd b. Abd al-Malik.

Meanwhile, Leo began his own march on Constantinople. At Nicomedia he easily defeated a small army sent to confront him under the command of Theodosius III's son and namesake, taking him prisoner with all his household, and then marched to Chrysopolis. Rather than risking a siege, Leo approached the Patriarch and Senate to open negotiations. The powerbrokers at the heart of the imperial system were under no illusions about which of the two contenders for the throne was better qualified to lead the empire through its impending trial at the hands of the caliphate. Theodosius III abdicated, retiring to a monastery, departing the capital on 25 March 717. His successor entered the city by the Golden Gate that same day, and was crowned Basileus Leo III in St Sophia. As promised, Artabasdos was promoted to the position of *kouropalates* and consummated his marriage to Leo III's daughter, Anna, making him son-in-law to the new emperor.

According to the *Chronicle of 1234*:

When Maslama heard that Leo had become emperor, he was overjoyed, supposing that he would thereby find an opportunity to fulfil his promise and deliver the city to him. And Leo, from the moment of his elevation to the throne, wrote constantly to Maslama, encouraging him in his vain hopes. At the same time, he was restoring and strengthening the city and gathering into it plenty of supplies. He was also having ships prepared for combat with the enemy. And he came to a financial arrangement with the Bulgars, by which they agreed to help the city. In short, he took every possible precaution to ensure the city's impregnability.

With the arrival of the summer campaign season, Maslama finalized his preparations for the advance on Constantinople. We can assume Sulaymān left Bakhtari in command at Chalcedon in order to report to Maslama, who then appointed him to take charge of the fleet from Hubayra. In June, Maslama pressed forward to Abydos, where he crossed the Hellespont into Thrace. The Byzantines did not contest his advance, Leo being content to undertake a scorched-earth policy on the Arab route of march. However, according to the *Chronicle of 1234*, after allowing the rest of the column to pass by, the Bulgars sought to wipe out the 4,000-strong cavalry rearguard under the personal command of Maslama himself; in a daring night assault, 'the Bulgar allies of the Romans fell upon him unexpectedly and slaughtered most of the force that was with him. Maslama [only] escaped by a hair's breadth.' This is corroborated by al-Ṭabarī, who records that the Bulgars 'attacked Maslama b. 'Abd al-Malik when he was short of men'.

On 15 August 717 the Umayyad host arrived under the walls of Constantinople. Maslama set up his headquarters in the suburb of the Hebdomon, so called because the area was situated exactly seven miles from the Milium in the forum of Constantine, from which the Byzantines measured distances along their roads. On the shore of the Bosporus, the Hebdomon stretched from the Cyclobium, the circular tower on its eastern headland,

The Theodosian land walls were constructed of alternating layers of stone and brick. The bricks are sometimes stamped with the name of their manufacturer or donor, perhaps giving some indication of where they were manufactured, or the name of the contemporary emperor. This enables archaeologists to date when repairs or restoration projects were carried out. Note the topmost inscription in this series begins with the word *nika* – victory. (Author's collection)

The Galata Bridge today spans the Golden Horn, so called 'from the similarity of the shape', in the account of Dionysius of Byzantium: 'It surpasses a gulf in depth … and a harbour in convenience.' The bridge roughly follows the line of the great chain that stretched from Constantinople to the suburb of Galata on the north shore of the Golden Horn. (Author's collection)

to the Magnaura at its western extremity, and included two palaces, the Castellum of the Theodosians, and the Jucundiana built by Justinian I, which were used as summer residences by the emperors.

Having set up camp, Maslama immediately placed the city under siege; 'he blockaded the inhabitants and attacked them with siege-engines', the *Kitāb al-'Uyun* relates. To cut Constantinople off by land, the Arabs set up a line of circumvallation by digging a trench opposite the Theodosian walls and erecting above it a barricade of rough stone. The Arab siege lines extended to the shore on the far side of Constantinople in order to incorporate the fortified suburb of Galata, which anchored the northern end of the great chain protecting the entrance to the Golden Horn. In this sector Umayyad patrols were kept on their toes by Byzantine raiding parties, 'who tried to draw them off and to prevent supplies from reaching the Arabs', according to the *Chronicle of 1234*.

To protect their rear, the Arabs established a line of contravallation, 'while also punishing the Thracian fortresses,' Theophanes notes, in a bid to eliminate these Byzantine attacks on his outlying detachments or foraging parties. But Maslama's real concern was the threat of the Bulgars, whose looming presence in Thrace weighed heavily on his mind. Their raids and ambushes were an endemic irritant, but their ultimate intentions were opaque. Were they mustering their clans for a decisive assault on his position? The prospect of the Arabs being crushed against the city walls by a Bulgar onslaught would have helped keep spirits high in Constantinople, and no doubt Byzantine agents – and gold – were circulating in Pliska, seeking to inveigle the khan into more direct intervention on their behalf. If there was ever an Umayyad embassy to argue the caliph's case, the sources are silent. If there was no attempt at arriving at a diplomatic modus vivendi, it was a critical omission, for a Bulgar/Umayyad alliance might well have proved irresistible. Clearly, if the Bulgars did choose to tip the scales, their only motive would be self-interest, but where did this lie? From their perspective, was it better to preserve a weak Byzantine state as a buffer against the rising power of Islam, allow Constantinople to fall so as to absorb whatever fragments of the empire could be snapped up in the aftermath, or stand back and let both powers bleed each other into impotence? Taking no chances, Maslama stationed 20,000 men under Sharahil b. 'Abd to guard against any threat to his rear throughout the siege. This deployment proved its worth when, according to the *Chronicle of 1234*, 'the Bulgars gathered against Sharahil and his army, did battle with them, and killed a large number of them, so that the Arabs came to fear the Bulgars more than the Romans'.

Maslama also sent out foraging parties, which returned in wagons weighed down with grain 'until that which was brought to him became like mountains, and these stores abounded in his camp,' the *Kitāb al-'Uyun* relates. As Maslama anticipated a long siege, al-Ṭabarī notes, this stockpile was reserved for the winter, the army being instructed to sow the abandoned fields in order to reap the grains the following summer. In the meantime, 'the men ate of what they carried off in plundering raids'.

On 1 September 717, Sulaymān entered the Propontis (Sea of Marmora) at the head of the main Umayyad fleet, including both front-line ships and fighting merchantmen. Content to conserve their strength, the Byzantines made no attempt to contest his arrival. The fleet anchored for two days off the Hebdomon while waiting for the south wind to pick up. It then dispersed, some detachments crossing to the suburbs of Eutropius and Anthemios on the Asian shore opposite Constantinople, while others sailed north into the Bosporus, bypassing the city for their intended destination at Kleidion.

The intention was to cut off the approaches to Constantinople from the Black Sea as well as the Aegean. Ideally, a tight naval blockade would also confine the Byzantine fleet to the security of the Golden Horn. This would enable the Arabs to attack Constantinople along her sea walls, forcing Leo to detach units from the Theodosian walls, perhaps leaving them fatally undermanned and unable to resist a concentrated assault by land.

As the northbound Arab vessels passed by, Leo 'immediately sent fireships against them', Theophanes records, 'which turned them into blazing wrecks. Some of them, still burning, smashed into the sea wall, while others sank in the deep, men and all, and still others, flaming furiously, drifted as far off course as the islands of Oxeia and Plateia', the modern Princes' Islands located about 16km (10 miles) south-east of old Constantinople in the Sea of Marmara. 'Because of this the spirits of the city's inhabitants were lifted, but their foes shivered in terror, recognizing how powerful the liquid fire was.' This had tactical implications over and above its effect on morale, as Sulaymān that evening 'had planned to anchor at the sea walls and attack the battlements at the narrow neck of land', presumably in conjunction with Maslama launching an assault on the land walls. This attack never materialized. In fact, the Arabs were so intimidated by the Byzantine's secret weapon they refused to accept the bait when Leo raised the chain that protected the entrance to the Golden Horn;

The lead seal of the Bulgar khan Tervel, now in the possession of the Dumbarton Oak Museum. While modelled on Roman archetypes such as the shield and the spear slung over one shoulder, the impression created by the long hair is of a hybrid culture aspiring to the greatness of the Caesars but retaining its own sense of identity. The motto of the seal – 'Mother of God, lend Thy aid' – speaks to the personal conviction of the khan. His subjects would not convert until the following century. Note that the shield features a figure on horseback trampling a fallen victim. (ChernorizetsHrabar, CC BY-SA 4.0)

The battlements of the sea wall, facing south-west, out into the Sea of Marmara (Propontis). From this vantage, the defenders would have witnessed the arrival of Sulaymān b. Mu'ad with the Umayyad fleet on 1 September 717. (Author's collection)

'the enemy thought he wanted to entice them and would stretch it out again' when they had been lured into the narrow waters between the city and Galata. Sulaymān 'did not dare' take this gamble, instead moving the fleet north up the Bosporus to anchor at Sosthenios.

An invaluable resource in reconstructing the campaign is the eyewitness account of b. 'Asakir, who served with his brother, Abū Khurasan, in the Arab fleet at Constantinople; in his own words, 'I was one of those who went on military service in the name and on the payroll of 'Umar b. Hubayra when Sulaymān put him in command of the war at sea.' His depiction of combat during the siege indicates that the Byzantine stance was not passive but proactive. Leo, aware he would lose the initiative if his garrison continued to shelter behind the city walls, ordered detachments to sortie outside the fortifications. What ensued was a clash of combined-arms units in a war of manoeuvre:

> Maslama had drawn up the Muslims in a line (I had never seen a longer) with the many squadrons. Leo, the autocrat of Rūm, sat on the tower of the gate of Constantinople; he drew up the foot soldiers in a long line between the wall and the sea opposite the Muslim line ...
>
> I never saw a day more amazing for our advance by land and sea, the display of our arms, the display by the autocrat of Rūm on the wall of Constantinople and their array of this armament. They set up mangonels and onagers. The Muslims advanced by land and sea, the Rūm showed the same [manoeuvres] and fled disgracefully ...

This representation of Byzantine cowardice might in fact be a reference to the tactic of the feigned flight – Leo seeking to draw Arab infantry and cavalry within range of his artillery, and Arab ships closer to his Greek Fire-bearing dromons.

However, while Greek Fire had secured the naval perimeter of Constantinople, enabling the Byzantines to mass their garrison on the Theodosian walls, Leo could (or would) not gamble his fleet in a bid to break the Arab blockade by shifting to the offensive either in the Bosporus or the Propontis. His caution was strategic and logical. The imperial navy was still vastly outnumbered, and did not emerge triumphant from every ship-to-ship encounter, as documented in the account of b. 'Asakir:

> 'Umar and some of those from the ships were afraid to advance against the harbour mouth, fearing for their lives. When the Rūm saw this, galleys and light ships came out from the harbour mouth against us and one of them went to the nearest Muslim ship, threw on it grapnels with chains, and towed it with its crew into Constantinople. We lost heart. They came out against [another] ship to do the same; so b. Hubayra began to lament and say, 'Is there no man?' Abū Khurasan stood up and said, 'I am a man here; you have kept me in a ship with you as if I were useless.' b. Hubayra said to him, 'Go where you will; give what commands you like.' He pointed to a ship of the Persians whose energy and toughness he knew and said, 'Send me and my brother in a boat and command them to obey me.' Abū Khurasan ordered the captain of the ship to guide it to that which was carrying off the Muslims; but the captain was afraid so Abū Khurasan showed him his sword. He took his ship until it was alongside theirs; Abū Khurasan then bound them together with a chain so that neither could get loose from the other. We fought with swords from one ship to the other and the victory; we boarded their ship, put them to the sword and [the] commander who had done what he had done. He had thrown off his helmet and fallen on his knees, a bald-headed ancient. One of our men struck him without harming him so Abū Khurasan came forward and struck him a blow which split his head so that I saw that the blade had passed his chin, throat, and thereabouts. The rest surrendered; we led them to the Muslims near us and then went back to those who were of [the enemy] but they retired into the harbour.

Constantinople, therefore, remained isolated from Thrace by the Arab siege lines and cut off from its shipping routes to the Aegean, the Black Sea, and Anatolia. This meant Leo's capacity to communicate with, let alone govern, the rest of his empire was severely constrained, an important consideration given Umayyad reinforcements continued to traverse Asia Minor. Throughout the duration of the siege, a steady stream of contingents was dispatched from Dabiq to Maslama under al-Walīd b. Hishām, 'Abd Allāh b. 'Umar b. al-Walīd b. 'Uqba, and 'Amr b. Qays, thereby keeping the forces of the Armeniakon and Anatolikan Themes tied down on the frontier and unable to intervene at the capital.

Constantinople, therefore, had no hope of relief, reinforcement, or resupply. 'Maslama prosecuted the siege vigorously', the *Kitāb al-'Uyun* asserts, and the exigencies of the blockade 'pressed heavily' upon the city, for Maslama had 'excluded the inhabitants of Kustantiniyyah from all gainful occupation by land and sea'. Disaffection within Constantinople was the key to victory. Maslama may have surreptitiously entered negotiations with those partisans of Anastasius II, some of them high-ranking palace officials,

GREEK FIRE (PP. 66–67)

On 3 September 717, two days after rendezvousing with the army at the Hebdomon, the Umayyad fleet entered the Bosporus, dividing into its constituent squadrons to seek anchorage at the European and Asian suburbs of Constantinople. One division passed by the city heading north to make landfall on the shore between Galata and Kleidion. The intent was to cut Constantinople's communication and supply lines with the Black Sea. But as the rearguard (20 heavy ships with 2,000 marines) was passing the city, the southerly wind stopped and then reversed. The Umayyad fleet would pay the price for entering unfamiliar, and unpredictable, waters, as the Bosporus, according to Dionysius of Byzantium, is 'interrupted by the continuous, parallel protrusions of promontories, besides which there are continuous eddies and interruptions of the sea's flow. For the current, compressed into a small area and squeezed by the narrowness of the continents, flows down by fits and starts.' As the enemy vessels drifted towards the city, Emperor Leo III played his trump card.

The entrance to the harbour of the Golden Horn was protected by a great chain stretched across the water between Constantinople and Galata. Enemy ships dared not approach the chain, as they would have been exposed to fire from the Galata Tower, from the great Tower of Eugenius on the Constantinople side, and from the ships on guard from within. Leo now dropped the chain and unleashed his dromons (**1**), described by Sebeos as small, fast, and manoeuvrable vessels that 'might rapidly dart to and fro over the waves of the sea around the very large ships'.

In addition to their speed, the dromons were armed with the definitive Byzantine terror weapon, Greek Fire. This liquid (the exact composition of which was a closely guarded state secret) was stored in a pressurized vat below decks, which was connected to a bronze tube mounted in the prow (**2**). When an enemy vessel came within range, the gunner opened a valve that released the liquid. According to the *Taktika* of Emperor Leo VI, the liquid 'could be projected forward to left or right and also made to fall from above'. As it left the nozzle it passed over a torch and ignited 'with thunder and fiery smoke' (**3**), as Leo VI describes it. For additional psychological impact, these weapons were embellished with fantastical detail. In her *Alexiad*, Anna Comnena describes how her father, Emperor Alexius I, had the heads of animals or mythological beasts cast in 'brass or iron with the mouth open … so that it seemed as if the lions and the other similar monsters were vomiting fire' (**4**).

In an age of wooden naval technology, the effect was catastrophic. Greek Fire clung like napalm to any object it touched, and could not be extinguished by water. The Arab ships were immolated, along with their crews (**5**). Some sank with all hands; some crashed into the sea walls of Constantinople; while others drifted south by wind and tide until they washed up, still burning, on the Princes' Islands of Oxeia and Plateia. The spectacle was a tonic for the city's defenders, and sobering for the invaders, who would live under the shadow of death by liquid flame for the duration of the siege.

who remained unreconciled to the new regime; if Leo would not deliver him the city, perhaps they would.

Leo was able to win a breathing space by dispatching emissaries to Maslama seeking a ceasefire in order to open negotiations; 'they asked him to grant them a delay. And they conferred with him, and he gave them hopes of certain things, and they gave him hopes, and he remitted his attacks upon them; and in the meantime they on their part gained consolation and comfort.'

According to Arab tradition, Leo continued to string Maslama along with the pretense of being his stalking horse, covertly working to undermine resistance within Constantinople. He now advised his ostensible patron that, with just a single grand gesture, the imperial elite 'will hand over the government at one stroke'. Leo explained that the extensive preparations Maslama had made for the winter were actually sending the wrong signal, that the Arabs were resigned to a lengthy siege and lacked the stomach for battle. However, if Maslama destroyed his reserves of grain, the Byzantines 'will give up hope of your delaying and believe that you mean to fight'. Faced with this prospect, resistance would evaporate in two or three days, 'and you will take the city with very little trouble'. Incredibly, Maslama followed this advice, and gave orders his army's provisions be put to the torch. Even more remarkably, Leo asked Maslama if the citizens of Constantinople might first take a portion of the grain into the city, 'in order that they may see your good intentions towards them'. When Maslama granted his permission, 'Leo seized this opportunity, and in part of a day conveyed away a large quantity of the grain, and the hearts of the Romans were encouraged by the grain that they had with them and the burning of most of the grain of the Muslims'.

The defences of Constantinople, looking north in a restored section from the moat along the line of the outer wall. This rises some 3m above the present level of the *peribolos* and approximately 8.3m above the present level of the terrace between the outer wall and the moat. Its lower portion is a solid wall that retains the embankment of the *peribolos*. The outer wall ranged from 1.98m wide at its base to 0.6m thick at its battlements, rising some 3m above the present level of the *peribolos* and 8.4m above the present level of the terrace between the outer wall and the moat. The towers of the inner wall are 9.1–10.6m high, and are spaced out so as to alternate with the towers of the inner wall. (Author's collection)

Maslama then dispatched emissaries, including his key lieutenants Sulaymān and ‘Abd Allāh al-Battal to negotiate the terms of what they assumed would be the surrender of Constantinople. But now they encountered the true Leo: ‘Do you think that I will leave all that the emperors have collected in times past up to this day and come out to you? If I do this, I have neither intelligence nor religion.’ The emperor reminded them how the strategic balance had shifted: ‘I have left you no provisions or provender, but he has burnt it all at my orders; and you will perish in a short time, and there is no succour for you and no one to seek aid [from], and you have nothing.’ If Maslama was willing to abandon the siege and return to Syria, he would be granted safe passage through Byzantine territory. ‘But if he is not willing to do this, then he will meet with real war, very different from that in which he has been engaged.’

When the embassy returned to Maslama with this missive, ‘it dismayed and frightened him, and his wrath was extreme, and he was overcome by sorrow and great grief’. While he absolved al-Battal of any blame for this debacle, his suspicion fell on Sulaymān, who, anticipating the worst, ‘removed from his ring a stone that had poison on it, and he sucked it and died on the spot’. With his death, on 8 October 717, command of the fleet reverted to ‘Umar b. Hubayra.

It seems almost unbelievable that a commander so experienced and professional as Maslama could have been so hoodwinked as to carry out so self-destructive a policy; in the words of al-Ṭabarī, Leo ‘had confounded him by a trick with which a woman would not have been deceived’. At least – and at last – Maslama now understood with whom he had been dealing. When a Byzantine embassy subsequently offered to surrender the city at the price of a single denarius per citizen (another obvious ruse), Maslama replied, ‘No, by God I will take it by storm, or else Leo shall come out to me on the conditions on which he left me.'

Shortly afterwards, the winter of 717/18 arrived, and with it, the almost incessant north wind that sweeps off the Arctic, across the Black Sea, and down the channel of the Bosporus, bringing with it frigid rain, sleet, and hail. Theophanes records that snow blanketed the ground for a hundred days. The Arab army, bivouacked in tents over the summer, took what measures it could to seek shelter, constructing makeshift houses and, when the wood ran out, digging caves into embankments.

Consequently, al-Ṭabarī records how 'the Muslims met with hardships such as no one had ever met with before, until a man was afraid to go out of his camp alone; and the Muslims ate draught-animals and skins and the trunks and roots and leaves of trees – in fact everything except dust'. Within the Arab camp a measure of wheat reached the price of ten gold coins. Many soldiers walked down to the ships to tear off a strip of pitch just so they could have something they could chew on during the day in lieu of food. With famine came disease. The Arab army was ravaged by epidemics, and the frozen soil would not yield to burial, so hundreds of bodies were flung into the Propontis.

Relatively immune from the worst of the weather, the Byzantines, who 'considered the Arabs more imprisoned than themselves', were able to go over to the offensive, launching sorties under the cover of fog, snowstorms, and the long nights to keep the enemy constantly harassed and on edge. Throughout the winter, Leo 'pressed the Muslims hard in war, until they were reduced to great difficulties', the *Kitāb al-ʿUyun* records. The conditions wore down materiel as well as men. The ships of the Arab fleet, exposed to the elements, would have degraded to the point of being dangerously unseaworthy; many must have been sacrificed for the sake of their timber, their planks serving as firewood to meet the insatiable demand for warmth to stave off the incessant cold. Freezing, starving, disease-ridden, and relentlessly harried by their foes, morale in the Arab camp reached its nadir: 'Constrained thus on every side, with the spectre of death before their eyes, they abandoned all hope.' ʿUmar, concerned at the lack of information arriving from the front lines, dispatched an emissary to his field commander with instructions 'not to return without accurate information about Maslama and his army', according to the *Chronicle of 1234*. Maslama 'gave him a letter full of lies to take to ʿUmar, saying: "The army is in excellent condition and the city is about to fall"'. This failed to have its intended effect, for when the emissary returned to Damascus, he reported 'the very opposite of the good news contained in Maslama's letter. Then, indeed, the caliph shed tears and grieved deeply for the ruin of the Arab army.'

But Maslama held his force together throughout this ordeal, and conditions began to improve with the arrival of spring. The crops that had been planted the previous year could now be harvested, replenishing the food supply, and with the mountain passes open and navigation on the Mediterranean now safe, the Arabs could expect reinforcement, by land and sea.

First to arrive was a fleet of 400 ships, including transports and warships, under Sofiam, with men, armaments, and supplies from Alexandria. Shortly

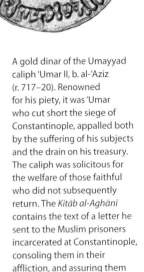

A gold dinar of the Umayyad caliph ʿUmar II, b. al-ʿAziz (r. 717–20). Renowned for his piety, it was ʿUmar who cut short the siege of Constantinople, appalled both by the suffering of his subjects and the drain on his treasury. The caliph was solicitous for the welfare of those faithful who did not subsequently return. The *Kitāb al-Aghānī* contains the text of a letter he sent to the Muslim prisoners incarcerated at Constantinople, consoling them in their affliction, and assuring them of his care for their families at home. (Noble Numismatics, https://www.noble.com.au/)

THE BITTER WINTER, 717/18 (PP. 72–73)

The Arabs maintaining the siege of Constantinople struggled to survive through the bitter winter of 717/18. As their foraging parties scattered ever wider across the already desolated wastes of Thrace, they became isolated and easy prey for a new threat rising behind their lines: Byzantine diplomacy – and gold – had coaxed the Bulgars into the fray.

The Bulgars were newcomers to the Balkans, and no friends to the Byzantines, with whom they had warred ever since crossing the Danube in the wake of the Slav migrations. An Umayyad–Bulgar alliance would have proved irresistible; with local support, the Arabs could have maintained a military presence in Thrace indefinitely, not needing to storm the walls of Constantinople to reduce the city to submission. But this never transpired. The Bulgars were looking to the future, and either because they considered the caliphate the greater threat in the long term, or because they aspired to claim Constantinople for their own someday, they were implacably hostile to the Arabs from the moment the Umayyad host crossed over into Europe.

The Arab rank and file felt the sting of this isolation truly begin with the first snows. Having exhausted their stocks of provisions, they were forced to forage ever deeper into an alien and unforgiving environment in search of sustenance. Depicting any given day during the long winter, the hunched forms of the gaunt, exhausted, and bedraggled members of this party are thrown into stark relief against the bare, bleak trees. Their uniforms are threadbare and covered in blankets, animal skins, and whatever else they have been able to scavenge, a vivid contrast to the gleaming, confident units that had mustered at Dabiq two years previously and marched proudly under the fluttering white banners of the caliphate against Constantinople. All they have accomplished in this bleak wilderness is to snare a couple of rabbits (1), an apt reflection of their ill fortune on this campaign in general. Either not expecting trouble, or too physically and mentally numbed by the cold to care, this foraging party is caught completely off guard by the sudden appearance of Bulgar raiders, who may have been stalking them for some time. The Arabs, startled, do not even have time to form a defensive line; the Bulgars cut them down if they stand to fight (2), and shoot them down or run them down on horseback if they try to flee (3).

The Bulgars are led into battle by their nobility (4), who are well protected in armour that embodies a hybrid style reflecting both their steppe nomadic origins and their inheritance in the Balkans. The common warriors following up in their wake (5) are more simply, but warmly, turned out.

thereafter, Yezid arrived with another 360 ships bearing reinforcements from Tunis.

A fresh army, under Mardasan, was also on the way, entering Asia Minor by the Cilician Gates and marching for Constantinople via Iconium. By the time the two relief fleets had entered the Propontis, Mardasan had advanced as far as Nicaea.

Both admirals had apparently been warned about the danger to be expected from Greek Fire, and in order to avoid contact with Byzantine naval patrols operating in the Propontis and the Bosporus, they approached Constantinople from the south-east, hugging the Bithynian coast of Asia Minor. Sofiam anchored his fleet at the harbour of Kalos Agros, while Yezid moored his ships at the harbours of Satyrus, Bryas, and Kartalimenos.

The commanders of the two fleets had taken every precaution, but there was one contingency they had not bargained for. The manpower demands of the campaign were such that the crews of their vessels were made up of Coptic Christian draftees and conscripts. Having made landfall, these men deliberated over their options and then elected to desert their masters.

The roots of this mass defection lay in the nature of Umayyad rule. The Copts had no love for the Patriarch of Constantinople, but the successors to Byzantine rule in Egypt had not delivered on their promised fiscal or spiritual autonomy. Administration from Damascus had led to the imposition of the *rizq*, an essential part of the supply system for the Muslim military imposed on the non-Muslim population, and the poll tax (*andrismos*), introduced at the time of the conquest and obligatory for all males over the age of 14. Additionally, after decades of détente, an Egyptian Copt, Severus b. al-Muqaffa, wrote of religious persecution beginning during the reign of the caliph al-Malik, when 'the Christians in the land of Egypt were troubled'. Tolerance for the *dhimmi* diminished further under al-Asbagh, eldest son of 'Umar b. al-'Aziz, the emir of Egypt and 'a hater of the Christians, a shedder of blood, a wicked man'.

The financial burden of the Umayyad war effort against Constantinople fell heavily on its subject peoples. Sulaymān had demanded his emir in Egypt 'milk the camel until it gives no more milk, but gives blood'. According to John of Nikiû, 'The yoke they laid on the Egyptians was heavier than the yoke which had been laid on Israel by Pharaoh.' The demands for naval procurement were especially enormous in Egypt, which had a long tradition of shipbuilding and producing fleets and sailors. Requisitions for the campaign were routine, and there was widespread conscription of sailors and skilled workers, like carpenters and caulkers.

Nevertheless, their decision to defect cannot have been made lightly. Should Constantinople fall, as traitors their lives would immediately be forfeit. But the price of victory would be to never see their homes or

The Mevlevi Gate (the Gate of the Rhegium) in Constantinople, between towers 50 and 51, was also called the Gate of the Reds, after the circus faction that built it. Constantinople's circus factions were as much de facto political parties as they were sports fans. Their tempestuous rivalry could create trouble for an emperor, or even bring one down if they were brought together, as nearly happened to Justinian. But their organization and energy could make them useful adjuncts to imperial rule, both in their contributions to infrastructure projects and as auxiliaries in defence of the city. (Author's collection)

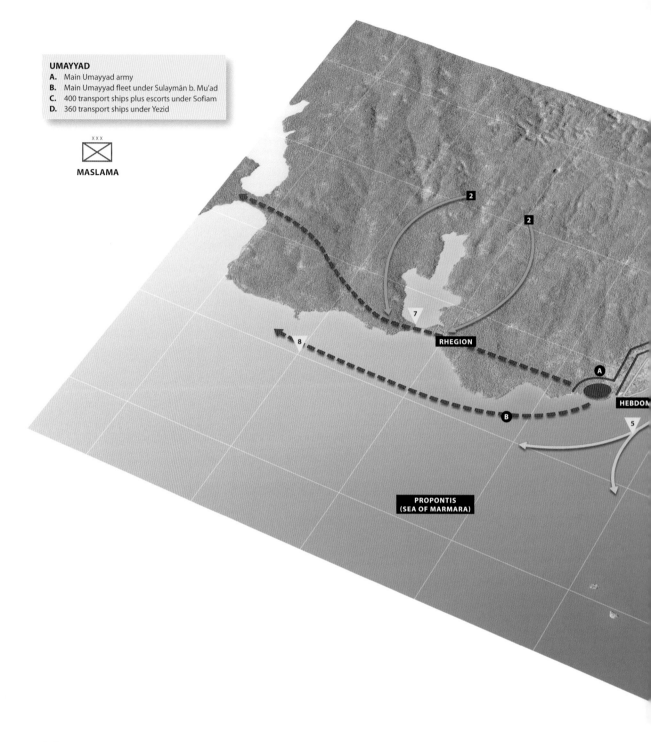

UMAYYAD
A. Main Umayyad army
B. Main Umayyad fleet under Sulaymān b. Mu'ad
C. 400 transport ships plus escorts under Sofiam
D. 360 transport ships under Yezid

MASLAMA

RHEGION

HEBDOM

PROPONTIS
(SEA OF MARMARA)

▼ EVENTS

1. Spring: Caliphal reinforcements from Alexandria arrive in a fleet of 400 transport ships plus escorts under Sofiam and anchor at Kalos Agros.

2. Spring: Caliphal reinforcements from Ifriqiyah arrive in a fleet of 360 transport ships under Yezid and anchor at Satyrus, Bryas, and Kartalimenos.

3. Spring: Christian crews serving under Sofiam and Yezid defect.

4. Spring: Leo III dispatches fireships and dromons to burn the fleets of Sofiam and Yezid and seize their cargos.

5. Summer: A caliphal army under Mardasan crosses the Taurus Mountains and traverses Anatolia to Bithynia opposite Constantinople on the Asian side of the

Bosporus. Leo III ferries Imperial troops to Bithynia; Mardasan is ambushed on the road from Nicaea to Nicomedia and routed.

6. Summer: The caliphal blockade of Constantinople is broken; with the remnants of the caliphal fleet confined to port by the ascendant imperial navy, the Byzantines are able to regain contact with the outside world.

7. 15 August: Maslama receives orders to abandon the siege. During its retreat through Thrace the caliphal army is ambushed by the Bulgars and loses 22,000 men.

8. Late summer: The caliphal fleet withdraws to cover the retreat of the army and link up with Maslama at Abydos. As the combined force withdraws, it is caught in a succession of storms and suffers massive casualties; only five ships return to Syria.

CONSTANTINOPLE, 718

The events around Constantinople, spring–late summer, 718

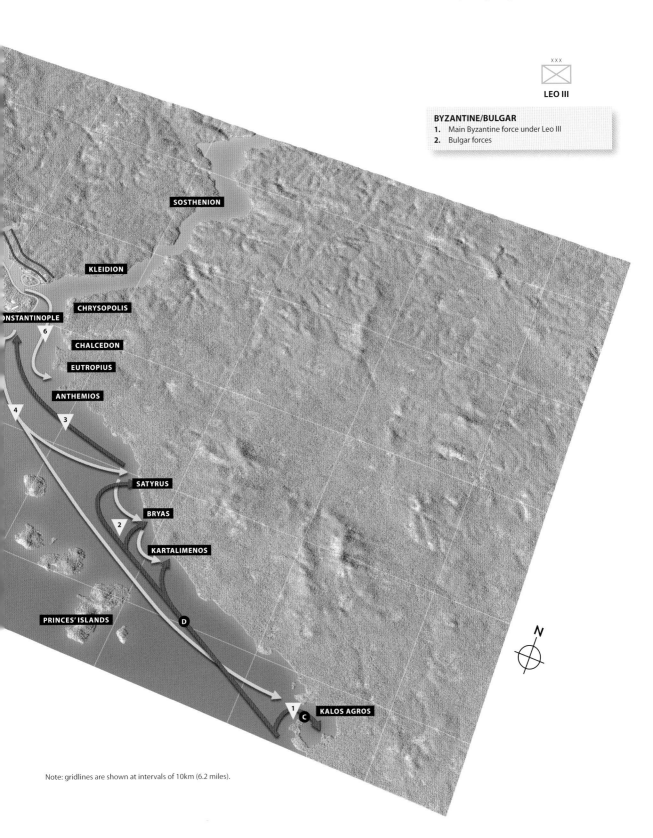

xxx

LEO III

BYZANTINE/BULGAR
1. Main Byzantine force under Leo III
2. Bulgar forces

SOSTHENION

KLEIDION

CHRYSOPOLIS

CONSTANTINOPLE

CHALCEDON

EUTROPIUS

ANTHEMIOS

SATYRUS

BRYAS

KARTALIMENOS

PRINCES' ISLANDS

KALOS AGROS

Note: gridlines are shown at intervals of 10km (6.2 miles).

The birth name of Emperor Tiberius III (r. 698–705), depicted on this gold solidus, was Apsimar, hinting at a Germanic origin. His reign was consumed with stemming the tide of the Umayyad advance in Anatolia. However, he failed to secure his throne against the threat from the west, as a Bulgar army restored Justinian II to power. The latter emphasized his authority by having the two former emperors Leontius and Tiberius hauled in chains to the Hippodrome, where he presided over the races with one foot on the neck of each of his prostrate foes, before having them dragged off to be executed. (Classic Numismatic Group LLC, https://www.cngcoins.com/)

families again. However, even after taking these realities into account, they were committed. 'That night they took the merchant ships' light boats and, acclaiming the emperor, fled to the city', Theophanes records; illuminated by the sentry fires on the city ramparts, there were so many small craft bobbing on the Bosporus, 'the sea seemed entirely covered with wood'. From them, Leo learned the locations of the two newly arrived Arab fleets, left immobilized and defenceless in the absence of their crews. He immediately unleashed the imperial navy, which plundered the stores and munitions on board the Arab vessels before torching all of them and returning in triumph to the city with the crucial spoils of this victory.

This annihilation of the relief fleets left Maslama bereft of a naval arm, as the vessels that had arrived the previous summer, left structurally degraded and chronically undermanned by the stress of winter, were in no condition to contest control of the water with their Byzantine counterparts. Leo was free to ferry select units of the garrison under the command of imperial officers (*basilikoi*) across the Bosporus to Bithynia. Here they linked up with the forces of the Opsikion Theme, which had played a key role throughout the siege by containing the naval bases the Arabs had established along the coast of Asia Minor. This joint force ambushed, and wiped out, the army of Mardasan between Libos and Sophon on the road from Nicaea to Nicomedia.

As a consequence of these decisive victories, the Arab blockade of Constantinople was smashed. The Bosporus and the Propontis were opened to Byzantine navigation; reinforcements and supplies could reach the city from Asia Minor, and fishing boats could ply their trade unhindered within sight of the Arab host ashore.

Having wrested back control of the sea, Leo could finally connect with the far-flung peripheries of his empire, which had effectively been operating in a political vacuum for more than a year. After losing contact with Constantinople in 717, Sergios, *stratêgos* of Sicily, 'along with the inhabitants of the West, gave up hope for the empire and the emperor himself on account of the enemy attack against them'. Sergios acclaimed one of his adjutants as Emperor Tiberius III, but this junta collapsed when the imperial *chartoularios* Paul, Leo's senior chancery official, arrived in Syracuse with news from the besieged Constantinople and reassured the people of Sicily 'that the Empire stood firm and that the City was confident as regards the enemy'.

This confidence was justified by the rapidly deteriorating situation in the Arab camp. Thrace had been stripped clean of provender, and nothing now could get through from Syria, Egypt, or Ifriqiyah. The besiegers had become the besieged, and famine conditions returned; according to Theophanes, the Arabs were reduced to eating the corpses of their comrades 'and their own dung, which they leavened'. Unsurprisingly, 'A pestilence fell upon them also and killed an infinite number of them.'

'Umar, who appreciated the strategic implications arising from the total defeat by land and sea of his reinforcements, decided the time had come to cut the caliphate's losses. He dispatched what additional munitions and supplies he could – according to the *Kitāb al-'Uyun*, 'clothes and provisions and horses' – but with them came an order for Maslama to abandon the siege and return to Syria. Aware of his cousin's indomitable fighting spirit, 'Umar gave specific instructions that if Maslama made any attempt to contest this command, the envoy was to bypass his authority and proclaim the order directly to the rank and file of the army. Sure enough, when the messenger arrived, Maslama immediately attempted to buy himself additional time, insisting he be given a few more days to reduce Constantinople, for 'I am on the point of taking it'. The messenger's reply was unequivocal: 'No, by God, not an hour.'

And so the siege was lifted on 15 August 718; in the Orthodox calendar, the day of Feast of the Dormition of the Mother of God; in the Islamic calendar, 13 Muharram, the first month in the year 100.

Leo would have permitted Maslama to withdraw his outlying detachments and conduct an orderly and unhindered evacuation in order to free Constantinople and its environs from occupation as soon as possible. Nevertheless, the Arab force would have continued ravaging and plundering the suburban and provincial areas throughout its withdrawal. However, vengeance was looming. Leo may have reached an agreement with Maslama

The luminous interior of the Hagia Sophia. Arabic tradition maintains that at the end of the siege in 718, Maslama negotiated with Leo in order to fulfil his oath that he would not depart without having first gained entry into the city. After giving orders to storm the city should he be detained, Maslama, clothed in the white of a pilgrim, rode into the Hagia Sophia on horseback, removed a gold cross, affixed it, upside down, to the tip of his lance, and, having completed this simultaneously insulting and triumphant gesture, departed. In fact, it would be more than seven centuries before Constantinople, and with it the Hagia Sophia, fell into Muslim hands. Testament to this final conquest are the great medallions (quoting the names of Allah and Muhammad, the first four caliphs, and Muhammad's grandsons Hassan and Hussein). (Filip Filipović/Pixabay)

The burial place of Abū Ayyūb al-Anṣārī, who served at an extremely advanced age in the siege of Constantinople. Struck down by illness, his dying wish was for his body to be laid to rest as close to the city walls as possible. His tomb was rediscovered after the Turks took Constantinople in 1453 and is now the centrepiece of the Eyup Sultan Mosque, one of the holiest shrines in modern Turkey. It is shown here on a winter day; the snowfall is a reminder the climate in this region is far from conducive to protracted siege warfare. (Sebnem Coskun/Anadolu Agency/Getty Images)

offering him safe passage out of Europe free of molestation from imperial forces, but this did not apply to the Bulgars. With or without Byzantine inducement, somewhere in Thrace, before reaching the Abydos crossing, 'the Bulgars attacked them', Theophanes records; 'and, as say those who know such things exactly, slaughtered 22,000 Arabs'.

Throughout the long retreat through Asia Minor, the survivors would have been systematically hounded and harassed by units of the thematic armies. Following established Byzantine tactical doctrine, these would have targetted the Arab outliers and stragglers when, loaded with booty, oppressed by fatigue, and without adequate rearguards, they crossed the Taurus Mountains on their return to Syria. 'Umar dispatched reinforcements with horses and 20,000 mules to escort the remnants of his army back into caliphal territory, for all their livestock had long since either been eaten or perished from cold or hunger. He also allocated ten gold coins per man, and issued a call throughout his domain to anyone who had a brother or other relative who had served under Maslama to take whatever provisions they could spare for their kinsmen's sake; 'Many did go out to meet them and did all they could do to save them.'

The remnants of the once formidable Arab armada, meanwhile, were scattered by a tempest in the Propontis as they sailed for home, and further battered by frightful storms, with thunder, lightning, and 'burning hail' in the Aegean, which destroyed all but ten ships, half of which were subsequently hauled in by the Byzantines. Of the more than 2,500 Arab vessels that had participated in the campaign, therefore, only five survivors ever returned to their home ports.

AFTERMATH

The campaign had culminated in an unprecedented debacle for the caliphate, and Leo was able to take military advantage. Within a year of the Arab repulse at Constantinople, an imperial fleet attacked the coastal town of Laodikeia (Latakia) in northern Syria and carried off the population, while thematic forces pressed into Armenia, the caliph fortifying Mopsuestia and Melitene against their pressure.

But Leo's priority was asserting full control over his empire, both in the provinces and in his own palace. That adherents to the former regime remained unreconciled to his legitimacy as emperor was vividly exposed in the immediate aftermath of the siege, when an attempted coup was orchestrated by a senior palatine officer, the *magistros* Niketas Xylinites. He plotted to restore the deposed Anastasius II by calling on the assistance of the Bulgars, who marched on Constantinople. But when the city failed to rise on behalf of the former emperor, 'the Bulgars handed him over to Leo and went home', Theophanes succinctly reports. Leo ordered the execution of his predecessor, along with the archbishop of Thessaloniki, the *protoasekretis* Theoktistes, the *komēs* of the Opsikion Theme Isoes, and Niketas Anthrax, the officer of the walls.

Further complicating the strategic picture, a new front opened up in the Caucasus in 724, when al-Jarrāh b. 'Abd Allāh al-Hakamī took Tiflis

The Madara Rider is a rock relief dating to the reign of the Bulgar khan Tervel; it may represent Tervel himself, the successor to the first khan, Asparukh. Tervel had a conflicted relationship with the Byzantine state, helping restore Justinian II in 705, who subsequently campaigned against Tervel. No consensus exists as to his subsequent role in Byzantine history. It is possible he died in 715; Theophanes records the treaty agreed with Tiberius III in 716 was negotiated by Tervel's successor, Kormesiy. If so, it was this third khan who intervened against the Umayyad siege of Constantinople in 717–18. However, Theophanes also records Tervel as playing a role in the factional machinations intended to restore the deposed Anastasius II in 718–19. The most plausible means by which to reconcile this discrepancy is to assume Kormesiy represented Tervel in the negotiations of 716 but did not succeed him until the traditionally accepted date, 721. (akg-images/Rainer Hackenberg)

The ongoing struggle, 717–1025

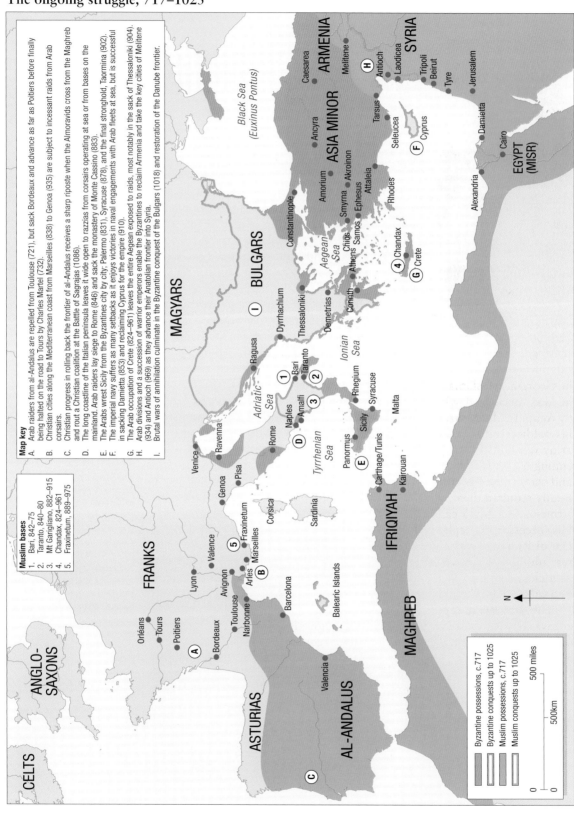

Map key

A. Arab raiders from al-Andalus are repelled from Toulouse (721), but sack Bordeaux and advance as far as Poitiers before finally being halted on the road to Tours by Charles Martel (732).

B. Christian cities along the Mediterranean coast from Marseilles (838) to Genoa (935) are subject to incessant raids from Arab corsairs.

C. Christian progress in rolling back the frontier of al-Andalus receives a sharp riposte when the Almoravids cross from the Maghreb and rout a Christian coalition at the Battle of Sagrajas (1086).

D. The long coastline of the Italian peninsula leaves it wide open to razzias from corsairs operating at sea or from bases on the mainland. Arab raiders lay siege to Rome (846) and sack the monastery of Monte Cassino (883).

E. The Arabs wrest Sicily from the Byzantines city by city; Palermo (831), Syracuse (878), and the final stronghold, Taormina (902).

F. The imperial navy suffers as many setbacks as it enjoys victories in naval engagements with Arab fleets at sea, but is successful in sacking Damietta (853) and reclaiming Cyprus for the empire (910).

G. The Arab occupation of Crete (824–961) leaves the entire Aegean exposed to raids, most notably in the sack of Thessaloniki (904).

H. Arab divisions and a succession of warrior emperors enable the Byzantines to reclaim Armenia and take the key cities of Melitene (934) and Antioch (969) as they advance their Anatolian frontier into Syria.

I. Brutal wars of annihilation culminate in the Byzantine conquest of the Bulgars (1018) and restoration of the Danube frontier.

Muslim bases
1. Bari, 842–75
2. Taranto, 840–80
3. Mt Garigliano, 882–915
4. Chandax, 824–961
5. Fraxinetum, 889–975

Byzantine possessions, c.717
Byzantine conquests up to 1025
Muslim possessions, c.717
Muslim conquests up to 1025

0   500 miles
0   500km

N

CELTS

ANGLO-SAXONS

FRANKS

ASTURIAS

AL-ANDALUS

MAGHREB

IFRIQIYAH

MAGYARS

BULGARS

ARMENIA

ASIA MINOR

SYRIA

EGYPT (MISR)

Black Sea (Euxinus Pontus)

Aegean Sea

Ionian Sea

Adriatic Sea

Tyrrhenian Sea

Orléans
Tours
Poitiers
Bordeaux
Toulouse
Narbonne
Lyon
Valence
Avignon
Arles
Marseilles
Fraxinetum
Barcelona
Valencia
Balearic Islands
Corsica
Sardinia
Genoa
Pisa
Venice
Ravenna
Rome
Naples
Amalfi
Malta
Panormus
Sicily
Rhegium
Syracuse
Carthage/Tunis
Kairouan
Taranto
Bari
Ragusa
Dyrrhachium
Thessaloniki
Demetrias
Constantinople
Corinth
Athens
Chios
Samos
Ephesus
Smyrna
Akroinon
Amorium
Attaleia
Ancyra
Caesarea
Melitene
Antioch
Laodicea
Tarsus
Seleucea
Rhodes
Crete
Chandax
Cyprus
Tripoli
Beirut
Tyre
Jerusalem
Damietta
Cairo
Alexandria

in Georgia. Maslama assumed command the following year, but in 728, he was ambushed while retreating through the Darial Pass; according to Agapius, the Khazars 'put him to rout, killing a very great number of his soldiers'. Al-Jarrāh was recalled to command on this front, but his army was annihilated and he was killed at the climax of a three-day battle ending on 9 December 730. Ardabil, the capital of Azerbaijan, was sacked and the Khazars roamed as far south as Mosul. Sa'īd b. 'Amr al-Harashī finally repulsed them, and Maslama was appointed emir of Azerbaijan and Armenia, waging a campaign of attrition until relieved on 3 March 732. His successor, his nephew Marwān b. Muhammad, drove north through the Darial Pass to surprise the Khazars, sacking their capital, Itil, in 737. The war ultimately petered out, with the Khazar khans converting to Judaism as a clear signal of their intention to remain independent of both empire and caliphate.

The Umayyad repulse under the walls of Constantinople was so comprehensive that Byzantine Anatolia enjoyed a brief respite while the caliphate recovered its strength. The interregnum was soon over, however, as incursions deep into Asia Minor resumed early in the following decade. In 721, the raids were led by al-'Abbās b. al-Walīd (who, according to Agapius, 'entered Paphlagonia, devastated it, [and] took into captivity 20,000 inhabitants') and 'Umar b. Hubayra; in 722, by Marwān b. Muhammad and 'Uthmān b. Hayyān al-Murri; in 723, by 'Uthmān b. Hayyān al-Murri and 'Abd al-Rahmān b. Salīm al-Kalbī; in 724, by Marwān b. Muhammad and the caliph's brother Sa'īd b. 'Abd al-Malik. In 725, the caliph's son, Mū'awiya b. Hishām, led a raid that penetrated as far as Dorylaion, while Maslama led a winter campaign that took Caesarea in Cappadocia by storm on 13 January 726. The summer of

Facing south-west from the battlements of the inner wall at Constantinople. The outer wall in this section is in particularly bad shape. During their joint rule, Leo III and his son and successor Constantine V repaired the Theodosian walls after they were damaged by an earthquake in 740. According to the *Parastaseis Syntomoi Chronikai*, 'the western walls, those of the great gates, were restored under Leo the Great and Pious'. Over the course of a procession to celebrate this achievement, 'the *demos* [circus faction] of the Greens shouted, "Leo and Constantine have prevailed!"' (Author's collection)

An impregnable citadel still sits atop the craggy pillar that looms over Afyonkarahisar, ancient Akroinon. After winning a decisive victory over the caliphate here in 740, Leo III renamed the city Nicopolis ('City of Victory'). The fact the Arabs were able to penetrate this deep into Anatolia in the first place – and not on a single occasion but repeatedly, year after year – speaks to the immense tribulation of the common people throughout the Byzantine Dark Ages. (Emin Başar ÖZDEMİR, CC BY 3.0)

that year was especially active, as Maslama, Mu'āwiya, 'Āsim b. 'Abd Allāh b. Yazīd al-Hilālī, and the caliph's uncle Ibrāhīm b. Hishām all commanded incursions.

The following year, provoked by the imposition of iconoclasm, the Themes of Greece and the Aegean islands 'rebelled against Leo in a great sea-campaign'. The insurgents approached Constantinople on 18 April, 'but were defeated because their ships were consumed by the artificial fire'. Taking advantage of this distraction, a massive Arab force penetrated as far as Nicaea; according to Theophanes, the vanguard 'went ahead with 15,000 light-armed men to surround the unprepared city, while Mu'āwiya b. Hishām followed with another 85,000'. But even after a 40-day siege and the partial destruction of its walls, the city held.

In 728, Umayyad naval strength – and confidence – had revived to the point where an incursion led by Mū'awiya was supported by a fleet under the command of 'Abd Allāh b. 'Uqba b. Nāfi. The following year, Mū'awiya and his brother Sa'īd b. Hishām led incursions by land that converged at Caesarea, supported at sea by a fleet led by 'Abd Allāh b. Abī Maryam. Mū'awiya led the raids of 730, 733, and 734; in 735, he pressed forward as far as Paphlagonia, while his brother Sulaymān b. Hishām fought his way through to Caesarea. Both siblings commanded incursions in 736 and 737, but this would be the last hurrah for Mū'awiya; after a storied career in which he 'captured many fortresses and took many prisoners', as Michael the Syrian relates, it was fortunate for the empire that while out hunting he 'fell from his horse and killed himself'. In 738, Sulaymān led one raid while another brother, Maslama b. Hishām, commanded the second.

In 739, caliph Hishām himself advanced to Malatya, while his son Maslama 'captured Ancyra and took many prisoners there'. In May 740, Sulaymān b. Hishām launched a massive invasion with 90,000 men dispersed across multiple fronts. According to Theophanes, following the 10,000 light-armed troops under al-Ghamr b. Yazīd in the vanguard, al-Malik b. Su'aib and 'Abd Allāh al-Battal led 20,000 cavalry

towards Akroinon while Sulaymān himself marched with 60,000 men to Tyana in Cappadocia. While the other Arab divisions 'withdrew unharmed after destroying a large number of men, women, and beasts of burden', the cavalry detachments under Malik and al-Battal 'were completely subdued and defeated by Leo and Constantine. Most of them, including their two commanders, were lost.' It was Leo's last triumph; he died the following year, on 18 June. The Arab summer campaign that season was again led by Sulaymān b. Hishām. His force was decimated by plague, subsequent to which the Byzantines 'put him to rout, massacred his troops', and drove him out of imperial territory. This was the decisive turning point. The Byzantines were able to go over to the offensive, and the caliphate itself ultimately collapsed, the Umayyad dynasts being succeeded by their Abbasid rivals.

It would have been fitting if Leo lived long enough to hear word of this victory. Having hurled back the best the caliphs could throw at him in the year of his accession, Leo had spent the rest of his reign fighting, year after year, to repulse endless Arab *razzias* in Anatolia; but never again would they put the very survival of the empire in jeopardy – and never again would they lay siege to its capital.

From an Arab perspective, the ultimate failure of the jihad could be interpreted as a consequence of applying the right lesson in the wrong context. In the wake of their great victory at Nāhavand, the Muslims had

Explicitly emphasizing dynastic continuity, this gold solidus displays Constantine V Copronymus (r. 741–75) with his son and successor, Leo IV (r. 775–80) on the obverse, and his father, Leo III, on the reverse. Constantine ruthlessly enforced the iconoclastic dictates of his father, leading to civil war with his brother-in-law Artabasdos, *stratēgos* of the Armeniakon Theme. A general purge followed Artabasdos' defeat by Constantine in May 743, during which Artabasdos and his two sons were publicly blinded in the Hippodrome. (Classic Numismatic Group LLC, https://www.cngcoins.com/)

Completed in 368, the Aqueduct of Valens was crucial to meeting the needs of the new, expanding imperial city of Constantinople. Fresh water arriving from a network of sources throughout the surrounding countryside could be stored in reservoirs and cisterns. Destroyed during the Avar siege of 626, the aqueduct was not reconstructed until 766, during the reign of Constantine V. The fact Constantinople could survive that span of time without this critical component of its water supply is a significant indicator of the extent to which the city's population declined during the Byzantine Dark Ages. This in turn eased the strain on the food supply created by the loss of Egypt. (Author's collection)

paused to consider their next strategic initiative in the east. Should they strike north against Azerbaijan, south into Fars, or straight towards the Sasanian capital at Isfahan? The direct option proved decisive for, as a Persian renegade advised 'Umar, 'Fars and Azerbaijan are the wings and Isfahan is the head. If you cut off one of the wings the other can work, but if you cut off the head, the wings will collapse. Start with the head!'

However, the conquest of the Byzantine enemy to the west may in fact have been facilitated by reversing this order and applying a peripheral strategy that first stripped the empire of her wings before ending with the head. The simple fact is, the grand campaign intended to land the final, fatal stroke was premature. The empire had not yet been worn down enough – physically or psychologically – to the point where the resources of the caliphate could be gambled on one decisive blow, which backfired spectacularly when its utter failure gifted the Byzantines space to recover. The caliphs would have been better advised to continue their incremental 'bite and hold' approach to permanently occupy territory in Anatolia and the Aegean, piece by piece, until Constantinople was completely isolated and reduced to the state by which she was described in 1453, 'a monstrous head without a body', ripe to fall.

In any event, as Maslama cast one last glance at the walls of Constantinople on 15 August 718, he may have had a Hadith, ascribed to Muhammad by 'Abd Allāh b. Muhayrīz, in mind: 'Persia is [only a matter of] one or two thrusts and no Persia will ever be after that,' the Prophet foretold. But the heirs of Rome 'are people of sea and rock; whenever a generation passes, another replaces it. Alas, they are your associates to the end of time.'

Ayasuluk Castle, overlooking the city of Ephesus. Once one of the great urban centres of antiquity, Ephesus, like most cities ringing the Mediterranean, declined precipitously during the Byzantine Dark Ages. The contraction of the money supply, the choking off of trade, and the constant Arab incursions made upholding the civic functions of a municipality impossible. Many cities shrank to the point where only a few diehards remained clustered in their final redoubts, whether fortified theatres (as in Miletus and Xanthos), temples (Didyma), or citadels (Priene and Ancyra).
(Author's collection)

THE ONGOING STRUGGLE

Now sole emperor, Constantine V worked to fulfill his father's legacy, both in enforcing iconoclasm and defending the frontiers. In 746, taking advantage of the factional divisions then wracking the Umayyad caliphate, he invaded Syria and captured Germanicia, his father's birthplace. The following year, the imperial fleet destroyed its Umayyad rival off Cyprus.

In 750, at the Battle of the Zab, the last Umayyad caliph was defeated by Abū al-Abbas al-Saffah, who founded the Abbasid dynasty. Still benefitting from Arab infighting, in 752 Constantine V led an invasion into the new caliphate, taking Theodosiopolis and Melitene.

Intensive incursions by the Abbasids commenced in 776. In 782, the caliph al-Mahdi ordered a massive mobilization for a campaign under the personal command of his son and heir, Harun al-Rashid. This force penetrated as far as Chrysopolis, from which Harun could gaze across the Bosporus at Constantinople. Abbasid raids began again in 797, reaching Ancyra that year and Ephesus the next.

The most massive Arab army ever to encroach upon imperial territory departed Raqqa on 11 June 806, with caliph Harun al-Rashid at its head. Herakleia fell after a month-long siege; the city was sacked before being razed, its inhabitants enslaved and deported to the caliphate. Caliph al-Mu'tasim personally led a major campaign in 838, sacking Ancyra and then marching on Amorium. According to Michael the Syrian, after the Arabs brought down a section of the walls, the defenders piled the bodies of the dead into the breach, 'so that it was filled in with corpses, and the besiegers were not able to enter'. But the city was betrayed and subjected

As Ephesus declined, the Byzantines built Ayasuluk Castle on the hill above the city. So much construction material was available from abandoned buildings that the outer walls were built 4m thick. Defensive walls reaching down from the castle encompassed the Basilica of St John at a lower elevation on the slope, effectively rendering the entire site into a citadel, with walls 1.5km around and boasting 17 towers. (Author's collection)

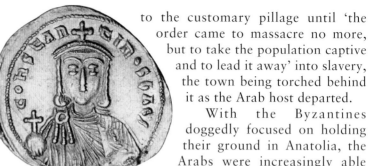

to the customary pillage until 'the order came to massacre no more, but to take the population captive and to lead it away' into slavery, the town being torched behind it as the Arab host departed.

With the Byzantines doggedly focused on holding their ground in Anatolia, the Arabs were increasingly able to assume the initiative at sea throughout the Mediterranean. While the fleets of the faithful 'covered most of the surface of the Mediterranean,' b. Khaldun gloated, 'Not a single Christian board floated on it.' The major islands – Crete (827) and Sicily (902) – fell to Islam, and in 846, Muslim corsairs sailed up the Tiber and laid siege to Rome, looting and desecrating the basilicas of St Peter and St Paul. Arab corsairs established fortified strongholds at the mouth of the Garigliano River in Italy (882) and at Fraxinetum above Saint-Tropez (889) as jumping-off points for forays deep inland. One after another, the major coastal cities of Christian Europe were sacked and plundered: Marseilles (838), Thesaaloniki (904), Genoa (935).

The 9th century was the nadir of Christianity. Every year, Viking longships spread terror from the north, Magyar horsemen roamed at will out of the east, and Muslim corsairs wrought havoc from the south. With its back to the Atlantic Ocean, the pitiful remnant of Western civilization by 900 appeared destined for extinction. But the 10th century marked its revival. The Vikings and Magyars were accepted into the Christian fold, while as the Abbasid caliphate splintered, the impetus of Arab expansion was spent. Relentless campaigning in Armenia and Syria enabled the Byzantines to reclaim lost territories from Ani to Antioch. At the other end of the Mediterranean, the Christian kingdoms of the Reconquista slowly pushed south into Islamic Andalusia. Between these extremes, the city-states of Italy began to claw control of the maritime sea lanes away from their Muslim rivals, while the intervention of the Normans in the mid-11th century tilted the balance of power in Sicily decisively away from Islam.

Then, suddenly, all of this progress was dramatically reversed. As the Arabs faltered, the banner of jihad was raised aloft by Muslim peoples new to the *ummah* from Central Asia and Africa. Striking north from their *ribat* in the Sahel, the al-Murabitun (Almoravid) ascetics carved out the first trans-Saharan empire in history when they conquered the Maghreb and then crossed into Andalusia, shattering a Christian coalition at the Battle of Sagrajas in 1086. Even more critically, 15 years earlier, the Seljuk Turks had annihilated the Byzantine field army at the Battle of Manzikert in 1071, breaching the Taurus Mountain barrier that had held the armies of the faithful at bay for four centuries and rolling up all of Anatolia in the aftermath. From the wreckage of this disaster emerged a new emperor, Alexius I; his appeal to the West for aid would be seized upon in 1095 by Pope Urban II as the pretext for Christianity's first collective holy war. Jihad had at last inspired Crusade.

This gold solidus features, on the left, Emperor Constantine VI (r.780–97) and, on the right, his mother, Empress Irene (r.797–802), the only woman in Byzantine history ever to bear that title. Constantine was aged just nine years old when he succeeded his father, Leo IV. His mother reigned as regent, convening the Seventh Ecumenical Council at Nicaea in 787 that decreed an end to iconoclasm. When she proved unwilling to surrender her authority even when he reached his majority, Constantine had to seize power in 790, only to lose it when a series of military reverses at the hands of the Arabs and the Bulgars, coupled with his decision to divorce his wife and marry his mistress, led to his being deposed in 797; his eyes were gouged out so brutally he died several days later. A deteriorating strategic situation in Anatolia, where the frontier was coming under increasing pressure from the Abbasid caliphate, led to Irene being overthrown in 802 and banished to the island of Lesbos. (Noble Numismatics, https://www.noble.com.au/)

CONCLUSION

How decisive for world history was the successful defence of Constantinople? For centuries, speculation about the limits of Islamic imperialism has centred on the Battle of Poitiers in 732. In a famous phrase, Edward Gibbon illustrated the implications of an Arab victory:

> A victorious line of march had been prolonged above a thousand miles from the Rock of Gibraltar to the banks of the Loire; the repetition of an equal space would have carried the Saracens to the confines of Poland and the Highlands of Scotland. The Rhine is not more impassable than the Nile or Euphrates, and the Arabian fleet might have sailed without a naval combat into the mouth of the Thames. Perhaps the interpretation of the Koran would now be taught in the schools of Oxford, and her pulpits might demonstrate to a circumcised people the sanctity and truth of the revelation of Mahomet.

Karen Armstrong asserts the Battle of Poitiers was essentially meaningless because 'the Muslims accepted that they had reached the limits of their expansion by this date, and coexisted amicably with the non-Muslim world'. One wonders who had less interest in the 'limits' of Muslim expansion; Bakhtiyār Khalji when he conquered Bengal in 1204, Mehmet II when he took Constantinople in 1453, Suleiman the Magnificent when he seized Buda in 1541, or Hussain Nizam when he sacked Vijayanagara in 1565?

Equally spurious is her argument the 'Arabs felt no compulsion – religious or otherwise – to conquer western Christendom in the name of Islam. Indeed, Europe seemed remarkably unattractive to them: there were few opportunities for trade in that primitive backwater, little booty to be had, and the climate was terrible.' This perspective ignores the fact the frontier of Islam was always being propelled forward by the momentum of its own success. Once initiated, the penetration of Europe would have been accelerated by the conversion of local peoples acclimatized to the uncongenial weather, just as progress across North Africa was facilitated by conversion of the Berbers and expansion into Central Asia was driven by conversion of the Turks.

Had Constantinople fallen, the Umayyad caliphs would have styled themselves as the legitimate heirs to the Caesars, including the ancient demesne of Rome; they may even have advanced their banner from Damascus to the city of Constantine. In any event, their new neighbours, the Bulgars of the Danube, would have accepted Islam, just like the Bulgars of the Volga. With these new believers adding impetus to its momentum, within living memory of the Byzantine Empire's extinction the caliphate would have stretched from the Bosporus to the Baltic.

The Silivri Gate (Gate of the Spring) in Constantinople, between towers 35 and 36. Like all of the larger gates, it is a double gate. Note the entrances through both the inner and outer walls. Such multiple sequences of security were why 8th–9th-century Islamic scholar b. Khurdādhbah called Constantinople 'the greatest city of the Rūm and their refuge'. (Author's collection)

What if Constantinople had fallen? The year 900

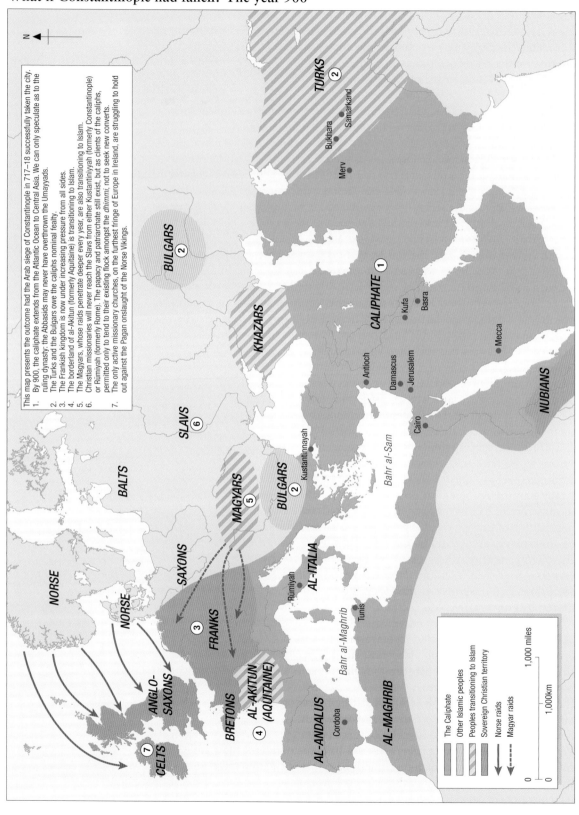

This map presents the outcome had the Arab siege of Constantinople in 717–18 successfully taken the city. By 900, the caliphate extends from the Atlantic Ocean to Central Asia. We can only speculate as to the ruling dynasty: the Abbasids may never have overthrown the Umayyads.

1. The Turks and the Bulgars owe the caliphs nominal fealty.
2. The Frankish kingdom is now under increasing pressure from all sides.
3. The borderland of al-Akitun (formerly Aquitaine) is transitioning to Islam.
4. The Magyars, whose raids penetrate deeper every year, are also transitioning to Islam.
5. Christian missionaries will never reach the Slavs from either Kustantiniyah (formerly Constantinople) or Rumiyah (formerly Rome). The papacy and patriarchate still exist, but as clients of the caliphs, permitted only to tend to their existing flock amongst the *dhimmi*; not to seek new converts.
6. The only active missionary churches, on the furthest fringe of Europe in Ireland, are struggling to hold out against the Pagan onslaught of the Norse Vikings.

TURKS ②

Samarkand
Bukhara
Merv

BULGARS ②

KHAZARS

CALIPHATE ①

Kufa
Basra

Mecca

Antioch
Damascus
Jerusalem

NUBIANS

Cairo

SLAVS ⑥

BALTS

NORSE

Kustantiniyah

Bahr al-Sam

MAGYARS ⑤

BULGARS ②

SAXONS

NORSE

Rumiyah

AL-ITALIA

Bahr al-Maghrib

FRANKS ③

Tunis

ANGLO-
SAXONS

BRETONS

AL-AKITUN
(AQUITAINE) ④

AL-MAGHRIB

CELTS ⑦

AL-ANDALUS

Cordoba

The Caliphate

Other Islamic peoples

Peoples transitioning to Islam

Sovereign Christian territory

Norse raids

Magyar raids

0   1,000 miles
0   1,000km

The Ottoman penetration of Europe, 800 years later, was not stopped until it was at the gates of Vienna, and the Sublime Porte had to fight its way through the centralized states of the Balkans and at least two crusades in the process; no such capacity for organized resistance existed in the 8th century. One way or another, the pagan tribes of the Slavs, the Magyars, the Lithuanians, perhaps even the Scandinavians, would have been absorbed into the *Dar-al-Islam*.

The consummation of this process is not difficult to imagine. With Anatolia and the Aegean under Arab control at one end of the Mediterranean, and al-Andalus at the other, the next logical step would have been to close the circuit by taking Italy. This was actually suggested; after conquering Visigoth Hispania, Musa b. Nusayr had proposed crossing Christian Europe from west to east, arriving in Damascus via Constantinople, in fulfilment of a prediction by the third *amir al-mu'minin* 'Uthman that 'Constantinople will be conquered from al-Andalus; if you conquer al-Andalus you will be partners of whoever conquers Constantinople.' A world where Leo III had lost his nerve, his city, and his head would have made this process that much easier. Coordinated caliphal columns converging from east and west by land, complemented with unchallenged Arab naval superiority, would have overwhelmed whatever resistance the Lombards, the Papacy, and any remaining Byzantine enclaves could have offered. The Mediterranean would thus have become an Arab lake.

The Yedikule Gate in the land walls of Constantinople. This was the smaller, civilian counterpart to the Golden Gate and handled the regular flow of traffic in and out of the city in this sector. Note the imperial eagle is still visible above the lintel in this photograph. It was stolen in 2009. (Author's collection)

The incorporation of Rome into the caliphate would have driven the Papacy into an uncertain exile, possibly shattering Catholic hegemony over religious dogma before it even began. Throughout the 7th century, 'the embryonic Celtic and the embryonic Roman Church contended with one another for the prize of becoming the chrysalis of the new society which was to emerge in the West', Arnold Toynbee observed. Had the Arabs been victorious at Poitiers, the frontier of the caliphate would have advanced to the Loire, cutting the Curia off from its flock in Western Europe. Accordingly, 'Western Civilization would probably have been derived from an Irish instead of a Roman embryo'. This outcome is even more likely in the event Constantinople had fallen; no one apostolic church, but rather multiple competing doctrines, further splintering the few remaining Christian communities of Europe.

The sum total of Christian realms at this point would have amounted to little more than the British Isles and the marginalized northern remnant of the Merovingian kingdom. The Arab attitude towards such pitiful fragments can be assumed from the protagonist of Harry Turtledove's alternate history *Islands in the Sea*, set in a Europe dominated by the caliphate after the fall of Constantinople: 'Let them be islands in the Muslim sea, he thought, if that was what their stubbornness dictated. One day, inshallah, that sea

The stairs leading up to the battlements of the inner wall at Constantinople were evenly spaced and broad, enabling more than one man at a time to sprint to his post in the event of an emergency. (Author's collection)

would wash over every island.' If the last Christian holdouts eventually came around to the true faith, so be it. The caliphs might have preferred they did not; a steady supply of *franj* taken as booty from the petty states of northern Europe would have been as welcome in the slave markets of the east as the *zanj* taken from Africa.

The long-term implications are of profound importance. Even assuming the ultimate disintegration of the caliphate, the successor states of Mediterranean Europe would have remained firmly within the Islamic economic and cultural orbit. While this would have empowered them to participate in the golden age of Islamic intellectual achievement, it also means they would have been assimilated into the fundamentalist backlash of al-Ash'arī, al-Ghazālī, and Nizam al-Mulk. Would this have aborted the artistic efflorescence of the Renaissance? Without this foundation, could the scientific inquiry of the Enlightenment and the technological breakthroughs of the Industrial Revolution have ever occurred? At a social level, without the separation of faith and state, could constitutional government and representative democracy have evolved? Could policies from the abolition of slavery to the emancipation of women have ever been contemplated? Horizons everywhere might be narrower. With no Reconquista, al-Andalus would have remained permanently linked to the markets of the East through sea-lanes spanning the exclusively Islamic Mediterranean. There would have been no incentive to develop the nautical technology necessary for navigation on the open Atlantic in search of alternate trade routes to the Indies. In such a reality, the heirs to the Mexica and the Inca might still govern to this day in the isolation of a New World never disturbed by the Old.

We can accordingly agree with the conclusion of Belgian historian Henri Pirenne that Leo's victory at Constantinople represented 'a historical fact of far greater importance than the battle of Poitiers'. Contemporaries – witnesses and participants – were under no illusions about the significance of what they had experienced. The Patriarch Germanus had recognized this in his sermon on the Akathistos Hymn, composed in the aftermath of the great siege:

> Our city had never before experienced threats such as these, indeed not even the most distant regions of the whole civilized world, where the name and polity of the Christians exists. For the whole body of Christ's flock would doubtless confess that it would have been at risk along with us if the Saracens who range themselves against the confession of His glory had attained the aim of their campaign against us.

In the game of history, therefore, the siege of Constantinople was played for the highest stakes of all.

BIBLIOGRAPHY

Belezos, Dimitris, *Byzantine Armies 325 AD–1453 AD*, Squadron/Signal: Carrolton, 2009

Blankinship, Khalid Y., *The End of the Jihâd State*, State University of New York Press: Albany, 1994

Bonner, Michael (ed.), *Arab-Byzantine Relations in Early Islamic Times*, Routledge: London, 2017

Brooks, E.W., 'The Campaign of 716-718, from Arabic Sources', *The Journal of Hellenic Studies*, Vol. 19, 1899, pp. 19–31

Cameron, Averil, and Herrin, Judith, *Constantinople in the Early Eighth Century: The Parastaseis Syntomoi Chronikai*, Brill: Leiden, 1984

Cosentino, S., 'Constans II and the Byzantine Navy', *Byzantinische Zeitschrift*, Vol. 100, No. 2, 2008, pp. 577–603

Crone, Patricia, *From Arabian Tribes to Islamic Empire: Army, State and Society in the Near East c.600–850*, Ashgate: Burlington, 2008

Decker, Michael, 'Frontier Settlement and Economy in the Byzantine East,' *Dumbarton Oaks Papers*, Vol. 61, 2007, pp. 217–67

——, *The Byzantine Art of War*, Pen & Sword: Barnsley, 2013

Donner, Fred M., *The Early Islamic Conquests*, Princeton University Press: Princeton, 1981

—— (ed.), *The Expansion of the Early Islamic State*, Ashgate/Variorum: Burlington, 2008

El-Cheikh, Nadia M., 'Constantinople Through Arab Eyes: A Mythology', in Angelika Neuwirth (ed.), *Myths, Historical Archetypes, and Symbolic Figures in Arabic Literature*, Steiner Verlag: Stuttgart, 1999, pp. 521–37

Enan, M.A., *Decisive Moments in the History of Islam*, SH. Muhammad Ashraf: Lahore, 1980

Foss, Clive, 'The Lycian Coast in the Byzantine Age', *Dumbarton Oaks Papers*, Vol. 48, 1994, pp. 1–52

Glubb, John Bagot, *The Great Arab Conquests*, Hodder and Staughton: London, 1963

Graff, David, *The Eurasian Way of War: Military Practice in Seventh-Century China and Byzantium*, Routledge: New York, 2016

Guilland, Rodolphe, 'L'Expedition de Maslama contre Constantinople (717–718)', *Études Byzantines*, Publications de la Faculté des Lettres et Sciences Humaines de Paris, Paris, 1959, pp. 109–33

Haldon, John, *The Byzantine Wars*, The History Press: New York, 2013

——, *The Empire that Would Not Die: The Paradox of Eastern Roman Survival, 640–740*, Harvard University Press: Cambridge, 2016

Hawting, G.R., *The First Dynasty of Islam: The Umayyad Caliphate AD 661–750*, Routledge: New York, 2000

Heilo, Olof, *Eastern Rome and the Rise of Islam: History and Prophecy*, Routledge: London, 2017

Hodges, Richard, and Whitehouse, David, *Mohammed, Charlemagne & the Origins of Europe: Archaeology and the Pirenne Thesis*, Cornell University Press: Ithaca, 1983

Hoyland, Robert G., *Theophilus of Edessa's Chronicle*, Liverpool University Press: Liverpool, 2011

Ibrahim, Raymond, *Sword and Scimitar: Fourteen Centuries of War between Islam and the West*, De Capo Press: New York, 2018

Jandora, John W., *The March from Medina: A Revisionist Study of the Arab Conquests*, Kingston Press, Clifton, 1990

Jankowiak, Marek, 'The first Arab siege of Constantinople', in Constantin Zuckerman (ed.), *Constructing the Seventh Century*, The Association des Amis du Centre d'Histoire et Civilisation de Byzance: Travaux et Mémoires, Vol. 17, Paris, 2013, pp. 237–320

Jeffery, Arthur, 'Ghevond's Text of the Correspondence between 'Umar II and Leo III', *The Harvard Theological Review*, Vol. XXXVII, No. 4, October 1944, pp. 269–332

Karapli, Katerina, 'The First Siege of Constantinople by the Arabs (674–678)', in Juan Pedro Montferrer-Sala, Vassilios Christides, and Theodoros Papadopoullos (eds.), *East and West: Essays on Byzantine and Arab Worlds in the Middle Ages*, Gorgias Press: Piscataway, 2009, pp. 325–36

Kaegi, Walter E., *Byzantium and the Early Islamic Conquests*, Cambridge University Press: New York, 1997

Karsh, Efraim, *Islamic Imperialism: A History*, Yale University Press: New Haven, 2007

Kennedy, Hugh, *The Armies of the Caliphs: Military and Society in the Early Islamic State*, Routledge: New York, 2001

——, *The Great Arab Conquests: How the Spread of Islam Changed the World We Live In*, Da Capo: Philadelphia, 2007

Khalek, Nancy: 'Dreams of Hagia Sophia: The Muslim Siege of Constantinople in 674 CE, Abū Ayyūb al-Anṣārī, and the Medieval Islamic Imagination', in A.Q. Ahmed, B. Sadeghi, and M. Bonner (eds.), *The Islamic Scholarly Tradition*, Brill, Vol. 83, 2011, pp. 131–46

Kobayashi, Isao, '"By His Upraised Arm God Saved the City": Byzantine and Arab Strategy in Mid-7th Century Asia Minor', in Takashi Minamikawa (ed.), *New Approaches to the Later Roman Empire*, Kyoto University: Kyoto, 2015, pp. 147–61

Konstam, Angus, *Byzantine Warship vs. Arab Warship: 7th–11th Centuries*, Osprey: Oxford, 2015

Nicolle, David, *Romano-Byzantine Armies 4th–9th Centuries*, Osprey: Oxford, 1999

——, *The Armies of Islam 7th–11th Centuries*, Osprey: Oxford, 2000

——, *Armies of the Muslim Conquest*, Osprey: Oxford, 2000

——, *The Great Islamic Conquests AD 632–750*, Osprey: Oxford, 2009

Norwich, John Julius, *Byzantium: The Apogee*, Penguin: Harmondsworth, 1991

Olster, David, 'Theodosius Grammaticus and the Arab Siege of 674–78', *Byzantinoslavica*, Vol. 56, 1995, pp. 23–28

O'Shea, Stephen, *Sea of Faith, Islam and Christianity in the Medieval Mediterranean World*, Holtzbrinck Publishers: New York, 2006

O'Sullivan, Shaun, 'Sebeos' account of an Arab attack on Constantinople in 654', *Byzantine and Modern Greek Studies*, Vol. 28, No. 1, 2004, pp. 67–88

Partner, Peter, *God of Battles: Holy Wars of Christianity and Islam*, Princeton University Press: Princeton, 1998

Petersen, Leif I.R., *Siege Warfare and Military Organization in the Successor States (400–800 AD): Byzantium, the West and Islam*, Brill: Leiden, 2013

Pirenne, Henri, *Mohammed and Charlemagne*, Barnes & Noble: New York, 1955

Pryor, John H., and Jeffreys, Elizabeth, *The Age of the Dromon: The Byzantine Navy ca. 500–1204*, Brill: Leiden, 2006

Qureshi, M.M., *Landmarks of Jihad*, SH. Muhammad Ashraf: Lahore, 1996

Stanton, Charles D., *Medieval Naval Warfare*, Pen & Sword: Barnsley, 2015

Stratos, Andreas N., *Byzantium in the Seventh Century*, Adolf M. Hakkert: Amsterdam, 1972

——, 'The Naval Engagement at Phoenix', in Peter Charanis and Angeliki E. Laiou (eds.), *Charanis Studies: Essays in Honor of Peter Charanis*, Rutgers University Press: New Brunswick, 1980, pp. 229–47

Treadgold, Warren T., *A History of the Byzantine State and Society*, Stanford University Press: Stanford, 1997

——, *Byzantium and its Army, 284–1081*, Stanford University Press: Stanford, 1998

——, *The Byzantine Revival, 780–842*, Stanford University Press: Stanford, 1988

Tritton, A.S., 'Siege of Constantinople', *Bulletin of the School of Oriental and African Studies*, University of London, Vol. 22, No. 1/3, 1959, pp. 350–52

Trombley, Frank R., 'The Arabs in Anatolia and the Islamic Law of War (*fiqh al-jihad*) Seventh-Tenth Centuries', *Al-Masaq*, Vol. 16, No. 1, March 2004, pp. 147–61

Tsangadas, Bryon C.P., *The Fortifications and Defence of Constantinople*, Columbia University Press: New York, 1980

Turnbull, Stephen, *The Walls of Constantinople AD 324–1453*, Osprey: Oxford, 2004

Vryonis, Jr., Speros, 'Byzantium and Islam: Seventh-Seventeenth Centuries', *East European Quarterly*, Vol. 2, No. 3, September 1968, pp. 205–40

Whittow, Mark, *The Making of Byzantium, 600–1025*, University of California Press: Berkeley, 1996

Yannopoulos, Panayotis A., 'Le Rôle des Bulgares dans la Guerre Arabo-Byzantine de 717/718', *Byzantion*, Vol. 67, No. 2, 1997, pp. 483–516

Zampaki, Theodora, 'The Mediterranean Muslim Navy and the Expeditions Dispatched against Constantinople', *Mediterranean Journal of Social Sciences*, Vol. 3, No. 10, July 2012, pp. 11–20

Zuckerman, Constantin, 'On the Byzantine Dromon', *Revue des Études Byzantines*, Vol. 73, 2015, pp. 57–98

INDEX

Figures in **bold** refer to illustrations.